Origins of the French Revolution

Socialist History 33

Rivers Oram Press
London, Sydney and Chicago

Editorial Board

Geoff Andrews	Nina Fishman	Kevin Morgan
Stefan Berger	Keith Gildart	Emmet O'Connor
John Callaghan	Karen Hunt	David Parker
Andy Croft	David Howell	Willie Thompson
Allison Drew	Dianne Kirby	Mike Waite
Elizabeth Fidlon	Neville Kirk	Chris Williams
	Kevin McDermott	

Editorial Advisers: Carlos Cunha, Eric Hobsbawm, Monty Johnstone, Boris Kagarlitsky, Gregory Kealey, Victor Kiernan, Stuart Macintyre, David Marquand, Lungisile Ntsebeza, Donald Sassoon, John Saville, Pat Thane

Editorial Enquiries: Gidon Cohen, School of Government and International Affairs, Southend House, Durham University, Durham DH1 3TG or gidon.cohen@durham.ac.uk

Reviews Enquiries: Matthew Worley, Department of History, University of Reading, Whiteknights, Reading, RG6 6AA or m.worley@reading.ac.uk

Socialist History 33 was edited by David Parker and Gidon Cohen,

Published in 2008
by Rivers Oram Press, an imprint of Rivers Oram Publishers Ltd
144 Hemingford Road, London, N1 1DE

Distributed in the USA by
Independent Publishers Group, Franklin Street, Chicago, IL 60610
Distributed in Australia and New Zealand by
UNIReps, University of New South Wales, Sydney, NSW 2052

Set in Garamond by NJ Design
and printed in Great Britain by T.J. International Ltd, Padstow

This edition copyright © 2008 Socialist History Society
The articles are copyright © 2008 John Callow, Gwynne Lewis, Peter McPhee, Stephen Miller, David Parker, Steve Pincus, Bill Speck

No part of this journal may be produced in any form, except for the quotation of brief passages in criticism, without the written permission of the publishers. The right of the contributors to be identified as the authors has been asserted by them in accordance with the Copyright, Designs and Patents Act 1988

British Library Cataloguing in Publication Data
A catalogue record for this publication is available from the British Library
ISBN 978 1 85489 1709 (pb)
ISSN 0969 4331

Contents

Notes on Contributors v

Editorial vi
David Parker

Rising Tides 1

The Rise of the Bourgeoisie and the Failure to Reform the
Bourbon State, 1763–92
Gwynne Lewis

The Absolutist State of Eighteenth-Century France 22
Modern Bureaucracy or Feudal Bricolage?
Stephen Miller

Revolution or Jacquerie?
Rethinking Peasant Insurrection in 1789 46
Peter McPhee

Perspectives 68
Forum on 1688
Steve Pincus, John Callow and Bill Speck

Books to Remember 102
Tom Nairn, *The Enchanted Glass*

Reviews 106

Notes on Contributors

John Callow is the Librarian of the Marx Memorial Library. He is the author of *The Making of King James II* (Stroud, 2000).

Gwynne Lewis, Emeritus Professor of History, Warwick University is the author of several books on the *ancien régime* and the French Revolution.

Peter McPhee is Provost of the University of Melbourne, where he has held a Personal Chair in History since 1993. His most recent book is *Living the French Revolution 1789–1799* (London and New York, 2006).

Stephen Miller is Associate Professor of History at the University of Alabama at Birmingham, his *State and Society in Eighteenth-Century France: A Study of Political Power and Social Revolution in Languedoc* was published in March 2008.

David Parker is Emeritus Professor of History at the University of Leeds, a specialist in seventeenth-century France, he is a member of the editorial board of *Socialist History*.

Steve Pincus is Professor of History at Yale University. His book *The First Modern Revolution* is to be published by Yale University Press in 2009.

Bill Speck is Emeritus Professor of History at the University of Leeds, and Special Professor in the School of English at Nottingham University. His most recent publication (with Tony Claydon) is *William and Mary* (Oxford, 2007).

Editorial

Revisionist historians appear to believe that socio-economic interpretations of the French Revolution and its origins have been vanquished by the sustained assault on them which began in the 1960s.[1] Until then the idea incorporated in both Marxist and liberal historiography that the revolution was produced by and to the benefit of a rising bourgeoisie was indeed largely uncontested. Successive waves of revisionists have since moved on from simply claiming that a capitalist bourgeoisie is hard to identify in the years prior to the revolution. According to some, the revolution was a political event produced more as a result of mismanagement and miscalculation; a political event, for those who have followed Francois Furet, which opened up spaces for new political forces bringing with them ideas of equality and democracy, and a reign of terror conducted against their perceived enemies. Furet's work heralded the arrival of avowedly cultural historians of a post-modern linguistic turn willing to detach the revolution from its social moorings. According to Keith Baker one does not have to do much more than understand the competing discourses of the Revolution (reason, will and justice) to understand the whole process.[2] The old notion that the Enlightenment was in some significant measure a bourgeois movement disappears from sight. Lynn Hunt's works moved from a preoccupation with the rituals and images thrown up by a new political class to a gendered interpretation in which the destruction of patriarchy, along with the monarchy, is central.[3]

Flanking the endeavour to transform the revolution into an essentially political and cultural phenomena without long-term, social or structural causes there is a tendency by historians who are in other ways far from revisionist to reduce or 'flatten out' the revolution by stressing the continuities across the revolutionary years. This is the explicit intention of Colin Jones's most recent and widely acclaimed work—an extraordinary attempt to exalt the reforming endeavour and effectiveness of a political regime which was in fact stumbling towards revolution.[4] Stephen Miller's article in this volume confronts Jones's argument with some of the abundant evidence which explains why.

Revisionism has certainly opened up some highly valuable areas of enquiry and stimulated much rethinking of revolution as a process. All our contributors would accept that 'the course of the Revolution cannot be deduced from its origins'.[5] But the broadening of the initial attack on the concept of a revolutionary capitalist bourgeoisie into a much wider attempt to belittle or just ignore socio-economic explanations has exposed major fault lines in revisionist constructions. This is partly because the classic interpretation of the Revolution did not reduce its dynamics to a class conflict between bourgeoisie and nobility. If the bourgeoisie were the ultimate beneficiaries of the revolution (which few gainsay even now) artisans and peasants played an absolutely critical part both as its allies and its opponents. The attempt to gut peasant rebellion of its class and radical content has largely faded out and Peter McPhee's article shows why.

It has also become apparent that the various revisionist tendencies do not cohere. William Doyle although a sceptic about the responsibility of the parlements for obstructing the monarchy and the significance of an 'aristocratic reaction' in the late eighteenth century is clearly made uncomfortable by the way in which what he calls the 'post revisionists' have detached cultural change from its social and economic context.[6] He was never in any event impressed by Cobban's judgments. Dale van Kley who has made a major contribution to our understanding of the cultural and intellectual climate in the pre-revolutionary years is similarly scathing about the flow of books from English historians which focus on eighteenth-century politics 'irreducibly defined as the play of personality and faction and the competition for power, position, and pension' with little regard for 'the role of ideas, ideology, or religion, treating politics as a more or less closed field of human action...'[7] Van Kley however happily notes the 'demise of the Marxian account of the origins of the French Revolution, and with it that of long-run socio-economic determinisms in general' making virtually no comments on the exclusion of social forces by these political historians.[8]

Ironically, Campbell's study of French politics, exempted by Van Kley from his strongest strictures, offers a view of the French state which not only puts a large distance between him and Jones, but in the process comes remarkably close to that which I myself offered in the very same year and which is confirmed by Miller's in-depth research; that is of a state apparatus changed little from the seventeenth-century and unable, as Campbell puts it, to cope with the demands of the later eighteenth-century world.[9] Whereas I rooted the limits of the absolute monarchy's reforming capacity in the social processes which gave shape to it, Campbell is content to describe the state as simply 'baroque'. In his introduction to a recent collection of essays on the origins of the Revolution Campbell ducks the problem posed by the affinities in interpretation by the simple device of ignoring them. This is a pity given his frank acknowledgment that revisionism has not produced agreement about the Revolution's origins.

It is also a pity that the collection, whilst including a quite un-revisionist essay by Markoff on the peasantry, does not address France's economic development. For if the original impetus to revisionism was a desire to destroy the idea of a rising bourgeoisie a powerful and equally revisionist current has sought to show that when compared with England, France's economic development in the eighteenth century was not as slow and limited as many thought. The jury is probably still out on what is a difficult and complex issue but enough indicators of progress have been unearthed by recent research to enable Henry Heller to assemble them into an unyielding restatement of the classic view.[10] Overdone this most certainly is—particularly in its insistence on a developing agrarian capitalism—but even those who stress the obstacles to capitalism recognise that the bourgeoisie, even if its capitalist component was not the dominant one, grew in numbers and in wealth. Moreover this view meets up with those cultural historians who recognise that the bourgeoisie played a significant part in the shaping of an increasingly autonomous public opinion and in the emergence of bourgeois values through salons, academies, libraries, clubs, cafes, Masonic lodges, newspapers, novels, painting and opera. Habermas's seminal work on the evolution of a bourgeois public opinion still has a resonance.[11] Jones and Doyle, despite their apparent revisionism, accept that culturally a bourgeoisie was in the process of formation even if the Revolution loses its old pivotal importance.[12] The article by Gwynne Lewis with which this volume opens offers some further thoughts about the processes which went into the making of the bourgeoisie and what really divides orthodox and revisionists historians.

It makes sense to incorporate in this volume the proceedings of the Forum on 1688 held under the joint auspices of the Long Eighteenth-Century Seminar of the Institute of Historical Research and the Socialist History Society. The demise of the French *ancien régime* cannot be explained without reference to the immense pressure exerted on it by England and the weight of this pressure cannot be explained without reference to the liberating effect of 1688. For too long a combination of disdain for the Whig view of the glorious and bloodless revolution of 1688 and the preoccupation with the real revolution of the 1640s reduced the significance of 1688—barely considered by the predecessor of the Socialist History society over the forty-three years of its existence. When revisionist historians stepped in it was to suggest that the changes which flowed from the fall of James II were the consequences of fortuitous circumstances which first allowed William of Orange to carry out a successful invasion and then during the 1690s give away much of the royal power. But over the last twenty years, despite efforts to minimise the industrial revolution and to emphasise the regressive features of a still aristocratic polity, a growing literature has offered a different perspective on the eighteenth century. All three of the opening speakers at the Forum insisted on the revolutionary nature of 1688 and, despite some not entirely compatible differences in emphasis, agreed on its progressive character. As the discussion showed, this approach and the terminology will raise important questions of both detail and interpretation; but they are surely the right questions.

One of these is how to assess the relationship between 1649 and 1688. It is perhaps surprising that that Marx spoke of the 'political supremacy' enjoyed by the English bourgeois 'since 1688', and of the 'new era' inaugurated by the 'landlord and capitalist appropriators of surplus value' brought into power along with William III. 'It is precisely with the consolidation of the constitutional monarchy' wrote Marx 'that the colossal development and revolution of bourgeois society begins in England'. What may surprise even more is that these references were dug up in 1948 by Christopher Hill whose overriding desire to demonstrate that a revolutionary transfer of class power came in the 1640s undoubtedly contributed to a prolonged under appreciation of the significance of 1688 for both British and world history.[13]

David Parker
University of Leeds

Notes

1. On the early revisionists, Cobban and Taylor, see Lewis below pp.1–4.
2. For Furet and Baker see Lewis below pp.3–6 and notes 8, 15, 17, 20, 21.
3. Lynn Hunt, *Politics, Culture and Class in the French Revolution* (Berkeley, 1984); *The Family Romance of the French Revolution* (Berkeley, 1992).
4. Colin Jones, *The Great Nation: France from Louis XV to Napoleon* (New York 1992), p.xii.
5. William Scott, 'From Social to Cultural History' in Peter Campbell (ed.), *The Origins of the French Revolution* (Basingstoke 2006), p.119.
6. William Doyle, 'The Parlements of France and the Breakdown of the Old

Regime 1771–1788', *French Historical Studies*, 6 (1970), pp.415–58; 'Was there an aristocratic reaction in pre-revolutionary France?', *Past and Present*, 57 (1972), pp.97–122; 'Reflections on the Classic Interpretation of the French Revolution', *French Historical Studies*, 61 (1990), pp.743–8.
7. Dale Van Kley, 'Pure Politics in Absolute Space: The English Angle on the Political History of Prerevolutionary France', *The Journal of Modern History*, 69 (1997), p.757.
8. Van Kley, 'Pure Politics', p.783.
9. Peter Campbell, *Power and Politics in Old Regime France, 1720–1745* (London, 1996); *Origins of the French Revolution*, p.13; cf. David Parker, *State and Class in ancien regime France. The Road to Modernity?* (London, 1996), particularly ch.7.
10. Henry Heller, *The Bourgeois Revolution in France 1789–1815*, (New York 2006), chs 1–3; for a more nuanced marxist assessment see Gwynne Lewis, *France 1715–1804. Power and the People* (London and New York, 2004)
11. Jürgen Habermas, *The Structural Transformation of the Public Sphere: An Inquiry into a Category of Bourgeois Society* (trans Thomas Burger. Cambridge, MA,1989).
12. Doyle, 'Reflections on the Classic Interpretation', pp.747-8; for Jones see Lewis, below, p.6.
13. Christopher Hill, 'The English Revolution by Marx and Engels', *Science and Society*, 12 (1948), pp.150–1.

Socialist History Titles
Requests for back issues to ro@riversoram.com

Previous issues of *Socialist History* include:

21 Red Lives
...Till Kössler on West German communists; Margreet Schrevel on a Dutch communist children's club; Tauno Saarela on characters in Finnish communist magazines...
1 85489 141 3

22 Revolutions and Revolutionaries
...John Newsinger on Irish Labour; Allison Drew on experiences of the gulag; Edward Acton, Monty Johnstone, Boris Kagarlitsky, Francis King and Hillel Ticktin on the significance of 1917...
1 85489 151 0

23 Migrants and Minorities
...Shivdeep Grewal on racial politics of the National Front, Keith Copley and Cronain O'Kelly on the British Irish in Chartist times; Stephen Hipkin on rural conflict in early modern Britain...
1 85489 155 3

24 Interesting Times?
...David Howell interviews Eric Hobsbawm; John Callaghan on reviews of *Interesting Times*; Ann Hughes on Christopher Hill's work; Cambridge communists reminisce...
1 85489 157 X

25 Old Social Movements?
...Meg Allen on women, humour and the Miners' Strike; Paul Burnham on the squatters of 1946; David Young on agency and ethnicity; Charles Hobday on the Fifth Monarchy...
1 85489 158 8

26 Youth Cultures and Politics
...Rich Palser on the Woodcraft Folk; Richard Cross on anarcho-punk; Michelle Webb on the LLY; Jonathan Grossman on apartheid...
1 85489 159 6

27 Rethinking Social Democracy
...Stefan Berger on the democracy gap; Andrew Thorpe on 'progressive' disunity; Aad Blok on Jan Tinbergen; Willie Thompson interview with Donald Sassoon...
1 85489 160 X

28 The Abyssinia Crisis
...Willie Thompson on Italian troops in Abyssinia; Christian Hogsbjerg on C.L.R. James and *The Black Jacobins*; David Howell on the 1935 general election in Britain...
1 85489 161 8

29 Collaboratiom, Resistance and the Unions
...Emmet OConnor on British unions in Ireland; Jonathan Jeffries on Gibraltar; Steve Cushion on the 1941 French Miners' Strike; Sarah Glynn on British Bengali politics...
1 85489 162 6

30 1956 and the New Left
...Lesley Hardy on E.P. Thompson and F.R. Leavis; Grant Pooke on Francis Klingender; Sebastian Berg on *New Left Review* and *Dissent*...
978 1 85489 163 1

31 Imperialism
...considers the changing nature of imperialism in the period since the Second World War...
978 1 85489 164 8

32 Activism
...lifts the lid on four different political organisations—the British Communist Party, the Labour Party, the Co-operative movement and the British Union of Fascists.
978 1 85489 169 3

Rising Tides
The rise of the Bourgeoisie and the Failure to Reform the Bourbon State, 1763–92

Gwynne Lewis

The main tenets of the 'Orthodox', social interpretation of the French Revolution were established at the beginning of the twentieth century by the renowned, socialist historian, Jean Jaurès.[1] However, this article focuses on the work of two of his successors, Georges Lefebvre and Albert Soboul. Lefebvre revealed the debt he owed to Marxist theory in two influential publications, *Quatre-vingt-neuf* (1939) and *La Révolution française* (1951). Albert Soboul, a member of the French Communist Party, was a more militant Marxist than Lefebvre. A résumé of his interpretation of the Revolution can be found in *Précis d'histoire de la Révolution française* (1962). The main reason for dealing with Lefebvre and Soboul is that they were chosen as the principal targets for the criticisms of Alfred Cobban ('Father of the Revisionists') in his influential anti-Marxist critique, *The Social Interpretation of the French Revolution*. Disputes over 'facts and figures' have rarely provoked serious argument between Orthodox and Revisionist historians.[2] It is the wider interpretation of empirical information that has always mattered, and this has far-reaching implications for the way revolutions, indeed, historical change in general, has been interpreted. A decade or so ago, Bailey Stone was convinced that Revisionist historians had 'shattered the old [Orthodox] socio-economic theory of revolutionary causation'.[3] This section will assess the validity of this assertion, with particular relevance to the debate over the rise of the bourgeoisie, and what Karl Marx actually wrote on this key question.

In 1964, the first edition of Cobban's *The Social Interpretation* reached the bookshops, eventually selling over 30,000 copies, and exercising a powerful influence over an entire generation of Revisionist historians. Its main objective was to confront the hegemony of the Marxist interpretation of the Revolution, at a time when the Soviet Empire was threatening America's position on the world stage. I have previously published a detailed critique of Cobban's main conclusions.[4] What follows is a brief commentary on three of the issues that are of relevance to this essay:

(a) The decline of feudalism and the 'rise of the bourgeoisie'

The issue of feudalism constituted 'one of the most famous episodes in the development of Marxist historiography since the [second World War]'—the famous debate on 'the Transition from Feudalism to Capitalism'.[5] For Cobban, feudalism simply did not exist by the late eighteenth century; the concept had only been invented by Marxists to sustain ideologically-charged hypotheses. He agreed that 'there was a widespread attack on something that was called feudalism', but this 'something', for Cobban, was the seigneurial dues that landowners levied on their estate. Cobban went on to argue that since feudalism itself did not exist then the notion of a 'feudal nobility' was 'a phantom'.[6] This was Cobban attired in his cavalier, crusading colours, seeking to destroy the Marxist concept of classes linked to changing modes of production. He accepted—for the sake of argument—that the traditional *bourgeoisie d'ancien régime* was expanding, but queried the Marxist contention that it constituted a 'class' related to socio-economic change. Even if it did, Cobban argued, it did not play a leading role in the overthrow of a [non-existent] 'feudal system'. He dismissed the idea that traditional *ancien régime* 'orders' and 'estates' were being transmuted, through the alchemy of 'historical materialism', into separate 'classes'.[7] We shall return to this critical issue later.

(b) The 'revolutionary' and the 'conservative' bourgeoisie

Cobban did concede that certain middle-class groups were involved in the outbreak of the Revolution, but he refused to accept the Marxist hypothesis of a link between 'the revolutionary bourgeoisie' and the advance of capitalism. He cited the conclusions of George Taylor, who insisted that pre-Revolutionary modes of capitalism had been 'built on the aristocratic and monarchic institutions of the old order rather than the urban industrial and financial system of the nineteenth century'.[8] Cobban, conscious of the need to find alternative hypotheses, went on to suggest that the revolutionary impulse really came from 'a declining group of *officiers*, holders of venal posts…' Unfortunately for Cobban, however, William Doyle's research proved that most judicial and administrative venal posts had, in fact, been appreciating, not declining, in value during the eighteenth century.[9] In section two of this article, we will see that leading ministers in Louis XV's government, men who actually ran the aristocratic and monarchic institutions of the *ancien régime*, were less attached to the 'old order' than most historians have suggested.

(c) The 'peasant revolution'

It will come as no surprise that Alfred Cobban believed that '"the peasantry"…is one of those vague formulas…that are hollow shells, meaningless or misleading unless some concrete content is poured into them. They are general omnibus terms'.[10] Nonetheless, Cobban went on to pose two interesting questions about the contribution of the French peasantry to the outbreak, and subsequent course, of the Revolution: (i) that 'the abolition of seigneurial dues was the work of the peasantry', and (ii) that 'it was the fear of the massive rebellion in the countryside, the Grande Peur, which forced the National Assembly to abolish feudalism'.[11] During the 1960s, even Albert Soboul, influenced by Russian historians such as Anatoli Ado, as well as by events in Latin America and Mao's China, began to support the concept of a '*bourgeois-paysanne*' French Revolution. Lenin had borrowed much of the agrarian policy of the Russian Social Revolutionary party in his sweeping revision of Marxism, and this encouraged Soboul to embrace a more 'Marxist-Leninist' interpretation of '1789', a significant move given the importance attached to precise ideological positions during the Cold War.[12]

Marx, Marxist-Leninism and 'Political Culture'

Alfred Cobban was a product of the political school of English history: he agreed with Professor Michael Oakeshott's conviction that History 'is an idiotic tale. The historian's god is chance'.[13] Matters pertaining to 'historical causation' were not fit subjects for respectable historians; teleological, historical 'laws', indeed, the 'social *sciences*' in general, were built on sand. In his *Social Interpretation*, Cobban states, categorically, that 'the *sans-culottes*, like the bourgeois, are not a social class; they are defined essentially in political, and not in social, terms'.[14] 'Classes', rising or falling, smacked of sociological theorising, as Cobban makes abundantly clear in two chapters of his book—'History and Sociology' and 'The Problem of Social History'. Once again, George Taylor was called for the defence: 'The French Revolution', he agreed, 'was a political revolution with social consequences and not a social revolution with political consequences'.[15]

Cobban bequeathed his empirical, political approach to an anti-Marxist, Revisionist tradition that continues to command widespread respect.[16] Two of the most influential scholars destined to continue the anti-Marxist campaign—Revisionism, second wave—were François Furet and Keith Baker. Furet was an acknowledged expert on Marxism, having been a member of the French Communist Party until 1956: Baker worked for many years with Furet at the University of Chicago. Both scholars, along with another conscript to the 'Chicago school', Colin Lucas, were responsible for the publication in 1986 of an influential, three-volume collection of papers, *The French Revolution and the Creation of Political Culture*. Furet acknowledged his debt to Alfred Cobban in an historiographical essay that includes words that might have been written by Cobban himself: 'We must return to what in history was explicit, which, in the case of the French Revolution, is to be found in its political history'.[17] Keith Baker reaches a similar conclusion: 'To understand the political culture of the French Revolution is to recognise the traces of the political culture from which it emerges'.[18] They all agreed that '1789' represents a momentous event in the history of Europe, if not the world; Furet went further, insisting that '1789' was the date that marked the beginning of 'modern political culture'.

Disagreement between Orthodox and Revisionist scholars became more disagreeable when discussing the relationship between 'changing modes of production', 'class formation', and the concept of revolutions as *necessary* agencies of change. Underlying all these issues is a fundamental disagreement over the adoption of political as opposed to social interpretations of history. In this instance, both Cobban and Furet adopted an uncompromising stance: the former, with one sweep of his pen, dismissed the entire foundation of Marxist epistemology: 'The desire for a general sociological theory, applicable to the whole of human existence, must…be dismissed as incompatible with critical history'; the latter also takes no prisoners, 'The French Revolution was, above all else, a laboratory of modern politics'.[19]

All this emphasis on 'political culture' is as myopic as vulgar Marxist insistence the importance of 'the economic'. We would argue that this blinkered approach only leads to over-simplification, and the fabrication of 'straw men'; it certainly distorts what the 'Young Marx', heavily influenced by liberal bourgeois historians such as Guizot and Mignet, actually wrote. For example, Cobban, reluctantly, was forced to concede that, despite accusations to the contrary, Albert Soboul did not believe that the bourgeoisie constituted a mature class on the eve of the Revolution: 'it was still diverse, it did not form a homogenous class'. If he had dug a little deeper, Cobban would have discovered that Marx himself believed that the French bourgeoisie was simply a 'class in the making' in 1789, and that the seizure of power by the bourgeoisie in 1789 was a 'political', rather than a 'social', event. Marx went further, arguing, that the bourgeoisie represented a *political* force that governed—especially after 9 Thermidor (27 July 1794)—in its own *political* interests. He describes the National Convention (20 September 1792–26 October 1795) as embodying 'the maximum of political energy, political power, and political understanding' in 1793.²⁰ For the 'Young Marx' at least, the seizure of power by the bourgeoisie in the summer and autumn of 1789 was a temporary, *political,* phenomenon.

The key to the confusion over these fundamental issues is to be found, of course, in the Marxist conception of the relationship between the 'political' and the 'social'. Marx prefigures Furet and Baker's arguments when he writes that 'The French Revolution, in overturning the *ancien régime,* created modern politics, a characteristic of market societies'. But this is where the two Revisionists and Marx part company, for Marx goes on to explain that 'since politics is an illusion produced by the alienation [a borrowing from Feuerbach] of "democratic" citizens in the new state, the French Revolution must in turn give way to a "real" revolution, one that will destroy the political by absorbing it into the social'. This is the central, 'revolutionary' message of Marxism. For Marx, a 'social' movement did not necessarily exclude politics, but 'there is never a political movement which is not, at the same time, social'.²¹ The ultimate act of revolution would be the universal social revolution of the proletariat, since the working class alone could break the chains of state and class oppression—for all classes. The Revisionist separation of the 'political' from the 'social' strips Marxism of its revolutionary potential; it also prioritises political and cultural history over social and economic history.

It was, of course, Vladimir Il'ich Lenin who really changed the terms of engagement between Orthodox and Revisionist historians, as Furet was well aware. Given the particular circumstances of the Russian Revolution—an historic event that hardly confirmed classic Marxist theory—Lenin concluded that he had no choice but to prioritise the 'political' over the 'social' ('grab history by the throat' rather than validate Marx's theoretical predictions). Christopher Read argues that it was during the long years of exile that 'the political Lenin took over to attempt the complete victory of his ideas and the political annihilation of his enemies'.²² 'Marxist-Leninism' would become the real *bête rouge* of the second-wave Revisionists. Cobban warned us that we could only understand the hidden message of Albert Soboul's influential thesis on the Parisian *sans-culottes* if we realised that 'current Communist theory is not Marxism but Marxist-Leninism'. Furet broadcast a very similar message: Leninism had 'enabled a glorification of the disruptive, creative, and almost demiurgical aspect of the concept of revolution, not just as a privileged form of action, but as its only valid form—at the expense of a concern for the objective conditions behind the historical events'.²³

We have described Keith Baker, François Furet, and their followers as second wave Revisionists, (a) because their work on political culture, involving 'discourse theory' and the 'linguistic turn', altered the terms, and content, of the debate between Orthodox and Revisionist historians, and (b) because, as the march of the Cold War invaded the streets and the classrooms, ideological differences became more overt. The battles that were fought between historians, especially after 'the revolution of 1968', were more personal, more institutionally based, especially in France. Furet provided the explanation: 'the historiography of the French Revolution during the twentieth century has been dominated in most European universities, beginning with the Sorbonne, by the Russian Revolution of 1917 and Leninism'.[24] And who was professor of French Revolutionary Studies at the Sorbonne—Albert Soboul. In Furet's penetrating, and personal, survey of the impact of communism on Europe, *Le passé d'une illusion*, Soboul, an eminent French historian and a militant communist, does not earn a single entry in the index. The nineteenth-century socialist historian, Philippe Buchez is given five!

The Catholic Monarchist 'Counter-Enlightenment' and 'the Making of the Bourgeoisie'

The adoption of a broader approach to the 'rise of the bourgeosie' enables us to follow new avenues of enquiry into the process of class formation, as well as new source materials for that enquiry. Sarah Maza has written that 'nowhere in the culture of pre-Revolutionary France can one find a substantial, conspicuous body of literature arguing for the separate merits, rights, or historical identity of a middle class or bourgeoisie'.[25] One obvious explanation for this apparent dilemma is that the records of a disintegrating, corporate society, founded upon 'orders' and 'estates', do not often contain 'a substantial, conspicuous body of literature' relating to a 'class in the making'. Class formation is a continual process, and, in the case of the bourgeoisie, as Marx pointed out, one that would not be completed, even with the Revolution of 1830. It is possible to discover, nonetheless, convincing evidence of an increasing degree of class-consciousness on the part of the bourgeoisie as the eighteenth century progressed. There are, for example, boxes of documents on 'the making of the bourgeoisie' in the *Bibliothèque nationale* as we shall see below. Colin Jones—supporting Jurgen Habermas's hypothesis of a link between a capitalist mode of production and a 'bourgeois public sphere'—has identified the later eighteenth-century *Affiches* as a 'discourse' of a market-orientated bourgeoisie that bought into 'a world of consumption, not corporate status'.[26]

This section of the essay concentrates upon a 'narrative', relating to the emergence of a bourgeois class, constructed by two eminent Catholic

Royalist reformers in Louis XV's administration—Henri Bertin, one of Louis XV's longest serving Secretaries of State, and Jacob-Nicolas Moreau, royal historiographer and a life-long friend of Bertin. Their joint objective was the reconstruction of the Bourbon monarchy after the calamitous experience of the Seven Years War (1756–63), a war that radically altered the political and economic priorities of Louis XV's government. It argues that, in their prolonged pursuit of this objective, they were obliged to entertain the possibility of a major transfer of political power from a declining feudal aristocracy to a new élite that would include members of the commercial and administrative nobility, but which would be increasingly dominated by the propertied, industrial, commercial, and cultured bourgeoisie. The 'omnibus' term *le peuple* would frequently be used to describe this new élite, but it would be a 'people' from which the property-less masses would be excluded, with dramatic consequences for the course of the French Revolution. As we shall see in the following section, the vision of *le peuple* held by these élites was fanciful, to say the least: 'It carried with it a justification for inequality and poverty'.[27] Bertin and Moreau were complicit in this historic act of deception, exploiting, as they did, the somewhat mythical view of the monarch as 'the father of the people'. In fact, when Louis XV died in 1774, the entire country breathed a sigh of relief.

The administration of the duc de Choiseul, which assumed responsibility for government in 1763 following the crippling defeat of the Seven Years War, embraced some of the ideas of the physiocrats who favoured the expansion of a more liberal free-market economy. Choiseul embarked upon a radical programme of economic reform, prompting one respected French historian to associate Choiseul with 'the birth of the Left'.[28] Henri Bertin had been appointed Controller General of finance in 1759. In December 1763, he was elevated to the position of Secretary of State, with a very wide brief that included the supervision of industry and agriculture. The policies pursued by Bertin and his friend Jacob-Nicolas Moreau would be geared to the reconstruction of a monarchy founded upon a new alliance of 'Throne, Altar and *le peuple*'; many of their ideas were associated with those of the 'Catholic Royalist Counter-Enlightenment', a movement that developed during the second half of the eighteenth century.

In an innovative study, Darrin McMahon suggests that some of the contours of the Enlightenment itself were shaped by the challenge of this 'Counter-Enlightenment'. For McMahon, 'the making of modernity' was a dialectical process, not a linear, triumphant march from Condorcet to constitutional monarchy. We will argue that 'the making of the bourgeoisie' would also be a dialectical process, shaped by its relationship with both the traditional nobility, on what would become the 'right-wing' of the political spectrum, and the popular masses on the left. The French Enlightenment was far from being the preserve of the emerging disparate bourgeoisie, especially when it came to spiritual and patriotic matters. As early as 1755, the General Assembly of Clergy had condemned 'the "contagion" being spread "throughout the realm" by the poisonous writings of "so-called *philosophes*".' Bertin and Moreau would seek inspiration from such unlikely figures as William Pitt the Elder, the champion of English patriotism, and the great Manchu Emperor of China, Kien-long, an absolutist ruler of a country with some 200 million inhabitants. They would participate in the new scientific debates of the age, rejecting the claim that the *philosophes* alone were the propagators of Enlightenment. In common with the great majority of their fellow 'anti-*philosophes*', they believed that certain principles were non-negotiable: 'If the *philosophes* assailed religion, then anti-*philosophes* must protect it. If the *philosophes* attacked the king, then his authority must be upheld. If the *philosophes* vaunted the individual, then the social whole must be defended'.[29]

Bertin and Moreau were convinced that, for the mass of the population, the Enlightenment of the philosophers was an exclusive club, run by wealthy intellectuals, frequently *seigneurs* like Voltaire, who cared little for the poor. In contrast, the anti-*philosophes* could cite the work of tens of thousands of Catholic priests and nuns who were dedicating their lives to the relief of poverty. It is all too easy to forget that 'The Roman Catholic Church in France before the Revolution was the most powerful organisation inside the kingdom, with a physical presence to match'. Religion may well have been 'the opium of the masses', but it still represented one of the major forces that would define the culture of France to the present day. The culture of Catholicism, and Protestantism, would contribute towards the making of the French bourgeoisie. For the aspirational middle classes, Catholic teaching, especially when clothed in its moral, Jansenist robes, was an attractive alternative to 'the licentiousness of the aristocracy' and the 'pornographic' writings of the *philosophes*. Dale Van Kley has argued that France was 'the only Catholic state where Jansenism put down significant lay bourgeois and even popular urban roots'. David Garrioch's detailed research on the *quartiers* of Paris validates the hypothesis of a link between the bourgeoisie and Jansenism.[30] For Bertin, and for Moreau (a fervent Jansenist), 'Church and State' were joined at the hip.

There is a rare archival source that reveals Henri Bertin's private thoughts on the dilemmas confronting the post-war Bourbon monarchy. It consists of a substantial collection of letters (the *Correspondance Littéraire*) exchanged between Bertin and French Jesuit priests in charge of a mission in Peking between 1765 and 1792, the year of Bertin's death.[31] The mission had been set up in the reign of Louis XIV, and was responsible for the propagation of the Catholic faith in China. Bertin would exploit their impressive store of knowledge, seizing the opportunity provided by the suppression of the Jesuit order in France during the early 1760s, to recruit the priests for his *Correspondence Littéraire*. Two young, Chinese Jesuit priests, Ko and Yang, who had been specially trained in France for the work of the *Correspondence*, were chosen to launch the venture. Before sailing from the port of Lorient in January 1765 for the ten-month return voyage to their homeland, they had completed a tour of French manufacturing and industrial sites so that they would be in a position to make useful comparisons with similar sites in China.

The *Correspondence* constitutes a veritable treasure trove of issues central to the Enlightenment, not just on the politics, economics and religions of China, but also on its cosmology, astronomy, hydrology, medicine, botany, philosophy, etymology, literature and history.[32] Bertin and his most gifted informant, Father Amiot, exchanged opinions on the relative merits of Chinese and French 'magnetism' as well as the efficacy of 'M. Sutton's inoculations for smallpox'; commented on a three-volume work by 'a M. Priestlys who has become celebrated through his discovery of different kinds of air'; and praised the publication, which began in the 1770s, of 600,000 volumes of the Chinese classics, history, philosophy, and literature which Bertin told Amiot was 'a truly remarkable undertaking'.[33] However, as the years passed, the *Correspondence* increasingly focuses on matters that are of more direct relevance to us—the formation of the bourgeoisie and the fall of the Bourbons. Louis Dermigny offers a plausible reason for this shift of emphasis. He argues that the attraction of China for both *philosophes* and anti-*philosophes* faded as:

> the ethics and exigencies of commercial capitalism began to make a real impact during the second half of the eighteenth century. Imitating China made some sense during the age of Louis XIV's confessional absolutism, but it was of decreasing value in the age of Louis XVI, when the 'rights of merchants' were increasingly being identified with the 'Rights of Man', and when French absolutism was being undermined by the rise of 'public opinion'.[34]

By the late 1780s, France, along with many other countries, was entering a period of economic recession, and this was having an impact on French trade in the Far East. On 10 January 1788, one of Bertin's contacts in

Canton wrote that 'while an increasing number of English ships were arriving each year, the French had recently lost control of the warehouse that had belonged to the old *Compagnie des Indes* (abolished in 1769, but revived, all too briefly in 1785).[35] By involving themselves in the American War of Independence, the French had been fighting the wrong battle in the wrong place. Both Bertin and his more famous protégé, Jacques Turgot, had been opposed to French involvement in the war.

In his extremely popular, distinctly Anglophobe, play, *The Siege of Calais*, performed in Paris in 1765, Pierre de Belloy drew a parallel between French success in the Hundred Years War and the national humiliation of the Seven Years War. The main message of the play is that patriotism alone can save a nation, but the significant point for us, is the emergence of *le peuple*, led by the bourgeois mayor of Calais, as the true saviours of France: the only noble character in the play, the comte d'Harcourt, turns out to be a traitor. *The Siege of Calais* was the script that dramatised the birth of Bertin and Moreau's 'New France'. For both men, the key issue for debate was the modernisation of the monarchy. They were hardly pioneers in this field. In 1748, Montesquieu's, *De l'Esprit des lois* had contained the alarming statement that only republican regimes could deliver *vertu politique*, respect for the law, and love of *la patrie*.[36] But Montesquieu was a spokesman for the nobility and the parlements (supreme law courts), and things had moved on since the flower of the nobility had been cut down at the battle of Rossbach (1757). Even the staunch monarchist, Jacob-Nicolas Moreau, had shifted his ground. In his influential journal, *Le Moniteur français*, he asserted that the monarchy would now have to engage more enthusiastically with 'public opinion'; that, in order to halt the political pretensions of the Paris parlement, Louis XV would have to adopt a more historical justification for the existence of the monarchy (Moreau would later become Louis XV's 'royal historiographer'!); and that, most surprising of all, the monarchy might want to reconsider its relationship with the nobility of the sword. Some of Moreau's ideas were evidently derived from the heated debate that followed the publication of the abbé Coyer's extremely popular publication of 1756, *La Noblesse commerçante*. Its main message, accepted in part by Louis XV's government, was that the nobility should involve themselves more in the emergence of a more capitalist and commercial society, an idea that appealed to Bertin, a robe noble whose family hailed from the world of industry and finance. He knew, all too well, that, in Britain, William Pitt, the Elder, had enabled the royal navy to 'rule the waves' on a tide of patriotism.

The trick was to 'democratise', without dismantling, a very unpopular monarchy. Attacking the traditional nobility, which had manifestly failed the people during the Seven Years War, did not seem to pose a major threat to their overall programme: it was hoped that the 'relics of feudalism' could be abolished without too much ceremony. Sadly, Bertin had underestimated the power of the parlements. One of the chief reasons for Bertin's dismissal as Controller General in 1763 had been his support for a land register (*cadastre*), interpreted by many nobles, robe and sword, as a revolutionary attack on the very existence of their fiefs. Nevertheless, in his new role as Secretary of State, Bertin continued to support, far more cautiously, the principles of free trade and a reform of the seigneurial system. Meanwhile, Moreau was devoting his time to the task of providing an historical justification for the existence of an absolute monarch, repackaged as 'the friend of the people', rather than 'the first among his aristocratic peers'. In his journal, *Le Moniteur français*, dedicated to *la Patrie et la Vertu*, Moreau denied that Bourbon absolutism contained any threat of 'Eastern despotism', since the sovereign courts, especially the parlements, acted as a check upon an overmighty king.[37] Despite the fact that both Moreau and Bertin were extremely worried about the *political* pretensions of the parlements, they believed that if the king shifted the basis of his power to rest upon a more enlightened, and empowered '*peuple*', then no 'intermediate agency', princes, nobles, or the parlements, would be able to take France back to the anarchic days of the mid-seventeenth-century *Frondes*.

However, Jacob-Nicolas Moreau's embrace of 'public opinion', his firm belief, constructed upon decades of research into French medieval history, that the monarchy should distance itself from the traditional nobility in order to move closer to '*le peuple*', represented a Catholic Royalist's reaction to the monarchy's loss of support—to stay the same, things would have to change! Marx could have been paraphrasing Moreau when he wrote 'that absolute monarchy appears in those transitional periods when the old feudal estates are in decline and the medieval estate of burghers is evolving into the modern bourgeois class, without [either] of the contending parties having as yet disposed of the other'.[38]

This was gist of the message that Moreau, supported by Bertin, delivers in a very revealing memoir commissioned by the city fathers of Périgueux (Bertin's home town) in 1775. The latter were seeking to defend their alleged status as a 'free city', free that is for wealthy bourgeois to buy noble fiefs without paying the traditional *franc-fief* to the Crown. Supporting their claims, Moreau's memoir denounces the 'feudal anarchy' of early medieval France and praises 'the burghers' of Périgueux for fighting, not only for their own freedom but also for the Crown, against rebellious nobles and foreigners. He also argues that towns were 'the cradles' of the bourgeoisie, which had secured their freedom by fighting the 'feudal nobility'. According to Moreau, the 'bourgeoisie' in the province of Guienne, particularly in Bordeaux (situated not far from Périgueux), had included 'persons of the highest birth... the most illustrious names, including those of princes, did not worry about being called bourgeois'. It was now time for the bourgeoisie's historic contribution to the monarchy to be recognised. Moreau wanted the bourgeoisie to join the robe nobility, as well as the abbé Coyer's *noblesse commerçante*, in a new political and economic power block. This new 'élite' would provide a counter-balance to the old *noblesse de l'épée*, thus providing a more stable foundation for a modernising, Bourbon monarchy. Clipping the wings of the second estate, (especially the peers and princes who could sit in the parlements), was an attractive proposition. Neither Bertin nor Moreau objected to the existence of a traditional, noble 'estate', they just wanted to break its *political* power'. Moreau would have appreciated Daniel Dessert's analysis of the problem: 'In a way, the bourgeoisie, as a socio-economic entity, was the involuntary daughter of the *ancien régime* state and its aristocratic society. The latter, however, if it could no longer subjugate this *classe triomphante*, could support it in order to benefit from the new economic regime, which, a priori, was not unfavourable to it.'[39] Moreau always refused to accept, or purchase, any noble title, an admirable qualification for a member of his new, moral, social élite.

Edmond Dziembowski suggests that Moreau's ideas escape 'every ideological classification', a perceptive comment that reflects the ways in which the Enlightenment was beaching many traditional ideological constructs. What he did detect behind the ideas of Moreau and the abbé Coyer is, 'the central question concerning the survival of the institutions of modern France. Could there be an accommodation between a political sphere, increasingly prone to rebellion against authority, and the principles that continued to preside over the destiny of a divine right monarchy?'[40] Moreau realised that boosting the image of Louis XV as a patriot was not enough. Given the legacy of madame de Pompadour's reign, a calamitous war, and the scandalous behaviour of Louis XV in his private brothel, the infamous *Parc aux Cerfs*, rather more was required to bridge the gap. He found it in 'religion and morality'.

Henri Bertin was a member of a very religious Catholic family; he had brothers who were either bishops or abbés, and sisters who were nuns. Some of the most compelling letters he exchanged with the Peking Jesuit priests reflect his persistent, and apparently bizarre, attempts to convince them that China, before the biblical flood, had been a colony of Egypt! This eighteenth-century 'creationist' interpretation of the bible was not as weird as it seems, however, given the widespread Enlightenment interest in history and etymology. Bertin appears to have converted the Chinese priest, Yang, who agreed that finding the true origins of the Chinese people was 'the key to the history of the world. M. de Guines [one of Bertin's 'experts' on this subject] has established the similarity of Chinese characters with Egyptian hieroglyphics'.[41] Moreau was a confirmed Jansenist. His father had been a Jansenist, and one of his brothers had been refused a curacy because of his Jansenist convictions. It is not surprising then that 'the first thing one noticed about Moreau was a moral, and moralising, tendency'.[42] It is difficult to underestimate the importance of public morality in an age of immorality, as the great success of Choderlos de Laclos's *Les liaisons dangereuses*, published in 1782, indicates.[43]

David Garrioch has emphasised the contribution of morality to 'the making of the Parisian bourgeoisie': 'The ideal of the *femme de qualité* and its male equivalent originated among a well-off middle section of society in search of an identity, which saw its own worth as lying in its moral qualities'.[44] As Marisa Linton has pointed out, François Furet's depiction of '1789' as 'the moment of a new "political discourse": one that conflated politics and morality' is as questionable as his general thesis on the outbreak of the Revolution.[45] Moreau had been conflating politics and morality from the 1760s. He believed that the collapse of the monarchy under Louis XV was due, in no small measure, to the king's sexual excesses, to his *moral* failings as a *Christian* monarch. With Moreau, we move from a biblical validation of monarchy, as supplied by Bossuet, to an historical validation: 'Few in pre-Revolutionary France grasped more clearly than Moreau the fundamental relationship between historical representation and political identity'. Between 1777 and 1789, he would struggle valiantly to justify absolute monarchy in no fewer than twenty-one volumes of his *Principes de morale, de politique et de droit public puisés dans l'histoire de notre monarchie* (note the order of importance: morality, politics, the law).[46]

Neither Bertin nor Moreau were working in a political and religious vacuum: pressures for a more nationalist and democratic form of political expression had been strengthening the Gallican foundations of the Church for decades. Following the attempt by Vatican agencies to take over the French Jesuit mission in Peking, Bertin launched an extraordinary, private attack upon the Papacy in his *Correspondence Littéraire*, only a few years before the Revolution. He told *père* Amiot that Rome had failed to meet its responsibilities, 'not only as a result of its poor choice of missionaries and the ridiculous and despotic type of government it wants to set up, but also by its preference for the *petites dévotions d'agnus dei*, rather than the great truths of our religion…I predict that not only will Christianity fail to make any progress in China but that it will be increasingly despised'.[47] This was the opinion of a loyal Catholic Royalist minister who had experienced something of a secular baptism in the waters of the Enlightenment, but he was not alone. Nigel Aston has detected a noticeable change of attitude towards the Vatican among traditional Catholics during the 1770s and 1780s. Rousseauist moralising became increasingly popular, even though 'The majority of Rousseau's readers were and remained Catholics'. Even the queen and her entourage paid their respects to Rousseau's tomb at Ermenonville in June 1780![48]

If many ordinary Catholics found a rewarding soul mate in Rousseau, Bertin appears to have found his in Confucius. The greatest Chinese sage, according to Father Amiot, had the answer to his friend's problems. Could there be a more revealing glimpse of the loss of faith in traditional values on the part of government élites? Ko had increased Bertin's interest in Confucius as early as 1770 by sending him translations of a few political and moral tracts relating to 'The Philosophy of the Confucian school, this philosophy that comes from the soul and is informed by *vertu*'. A few years later, Amiot informed Bertin that he was going to write a book on Confucius, a book that would take him until the end of 1784 to complete.[49] It must have delighted Bertin, since it suggested ways of governing a nation that was losing faith in its leaders. Amiot explained that Confucius, 'was one of the greatest Chinese philosophers; his simplicity, his candour, his modesty, his boundless respect for the ancients and the sages, *and even more important, for legitimate authority*, provides a striking contrast to the pride, arrogance, and spirit of insubordination that our modern philosophers display and emphasize in all of their works' [emphasis added]. This was music to Bertin's ears.[50] One year into the Revolution, Bertin would still be demanding more information on 'the doctrine of Confucius and morality'.[51] Is it possible that a dose of Confucian philosophy would have eased the angst of some liberal noble opponents of the government in 1788? Munro Price argues that such nobles were exhibiting 'disgust at a representational court culture that had signally failed to satisfy them materially or spiritually'.[52]

Class Formation and the Social Question

The failure to respond effectively to the plight of the poor and the dispossessed proved to be the single most destabilising socio-political problem confronting the Bourbon monarchy. It was a socio-*political* problem because the increase in poverty after 1763 was directly associated with the liberal free-trade measures introduced by the duc de Choiseul. We should note that the increase in poverty occurred during the 1760s and 1770s, a period often described as a 'golden age for the French economy', but it was also one that witnessed, in the spring of 1775, one of the most serious popular rebellions in the eighteenth century—the *Guerre des farines* or 'Flour War'. Certainly population growth and periodic, bad harvests had aggravated the situation in 1775, but, from Bertin in 1763 to Calonne in 1788, every Controller General expressed deep concern over the increasing number of popular rebellions. They form the essential background to the massive, politically charged revolts that changed the course of the Revolution from 1789 to 1792.

Under Louis XVI, roughly half of the population of Paris could be described as paupers in times of dearth, while, in the countryside, two to three million inhabitants lived on the wrong side of the ditch separating dependent from independent farmers. The majority of their offspring were lucky if they reached their first birthday: 90.8 per cent of the abandoned children farmed out from the Hôtel-Dieu to wet nurses in the countryside died before their first birthday.[53] Poverty was not a marginal issue, yet, as Jonathan Israel points out, mainstream, Enlightenment thinkers increasingly marginalised it. Voltaire ridiculed the seventeenth-century philosopher, Spinoza, for his belief that 'all men have one and the same nature; it is power and culture which misleads us'.[54] Moreau effectively disenfranchised the poor: their political role was to be nugatory: '*le peuple* are bound to their sovereign through their submission'.[55] What Moreau and Bertin feared was that democratic reform would lead to a social revolution that would sweep away the monarchy. They were right to be afraid! Mass poverty remains the most serious blight on the record of allegedly democratic, free-market, capitalist regimes.

The Great Fear of 1789, unique as it was in scale and political significance, did not mark the beginning but the culmination of serious peasant rebellion after 1763. John Markoff has identified a rising curve of popular revolt:

> From low levels during much of the century, apart from a spike around the famine of 1709, one sees clearly that the curve of conflict starts to rise in the 1760s. There is a sharp peak, the highest in the century so far, at the Flour War of 1775, and although the trajectory falls back afterward, it remains above its pre-1760s level and then begins a new, accelerating dizzy ascent in the late 1780s.[56]

Jean Nicolas and his team have produced detailed statistics on 8,528 pre-Revolutionary rebellions that occurred in France between 1661 and 1789. The team's analysis of the period 1763 to 1789 establishes the increasing severity, and violence, of popular rebellion. A new phase began in 1764, which, with brief respites, continued to the end of the century: 101 uprisings in 1766, 145 in 1768, rising to 226 in the spring of 1775 (the time of the *Guerre des farines*), and to 310 in the spring of 1789 (the Great Fear). These waves of rebellion affected towns more often than *bourgs* and villages—about 40 per cent urban, 20 per cent rural. Throughout the period studied, 1661–1789, anti-fiscal revolts (usually against indirect taxes) predominated. They peaked between 1763–1789, with 1113 riots (out of a total of 2779) directed against the salt tax (*gabelle*) and impositions on wines and spirits (*aides*).[57]

Between the 1760s and 1789, the official response to the increase of crime and popular resistance would vacillate between savage repression and virtual imprisonment in the new *dépôts de mendicité* or workhouses, although, during the peak crisis of the *Guerre des farines*, Jacques Turgot would create charitable work for the poor. The policies introduced by Choiseul in the 1760s, however, had represented an extension of the campaign against 'criminal disorder' that had begun with the 'Great Confinement' of the 1720s, a campaign which had also threatened the 'undeserving poor' with imprisonment, the galleys or the gibbet. Choiseul's reforms had included the establishment of 30 urban workhouses: they rapidly proved to be as unpopular as the workhouses described by Charles Dickens'. Unhealthy and underfunded, they were frequently the sites of periodic and serious rioting.[58] The causes of this 'rising tide of rebellion' are varied and complex; they include higher taxation, poor harvests, and the early signs of political maturity, but high on Jean Nicolas's list is widespread resistance to the introduction of liberal, free-trade policies. From the 1760s, successive governments choreographed policies that alternated between freeing the grain trade in times of surplus, and regulating it in times of dearth, a *ballet-à-deux* that would continue into the nineteenth century. A government edict in March 1765 had allowed the nobility to participate in the grain trade without loss of privilege, a striking indication of the way free-market capitalism was facilitating the creation of a new élite. Political economic change was also influencing class formation. In 1767, the Scottish political economist, Sir James Steuart, very impressed with the 'Choiseul revolution', provided an assessment of the changing times: 'Trade and industry are in vogue [in France]; and their establishment is occasioning a wonderful fermentation with the remaining fierceness of the feudal constitution'.[59] Marx, like Steuart, saw the physiocrats as promoters of liberal capitalism, but 'still in thrall to the feudal outlook insofar as they declared landownership and land cultivation to be that…which determines the whole structure of society.'[60] In fact, many physiocrats, from Quesnay to Turgot, were eager to root out the remains of a feudal land system, which explains why Marx described Jacques Turgot as 'a radical bourgeois'.

On 13 September 1774, Turgot announced that internal controls on the sale of grain would be abolished. The timing was unfortunate: following a harsh winter, the poor harvest of 1775 led to rising grain prices, which, in turn, provoked the *Guerre des farines*. The rich denounced the increasing intractability of 'the mob' (*canaille*); the rebels, almost 600 of whom were arrested, denounced 'monopolists', 'hoarders' and 'speculators'. The politician who would be called upon to save the conservative revolution of 1789, Jacques Necker, wrote in his pamphlet, *Sur la Législation et le Commerce des grains*, that, although legislation had been passed to control the masses and protect property rights, 'almost nothing has yet been done for the majority of our citizens'.[61] The Assembly of Notables in the spring of 1789 would construe Calonne's radical blueprint for change as an *appel au peuple*, one that was capable of breaking 'the invisible chain which links all citizens to their duty of obedience'.[62] During the Revolution, the urban and rural poor would act within a very different political and ideological context, one that would enable them to achieve their own immediate objectives—the abolition of the *ancien régime* seigneurial and fiscal systems.

On 11 May 1789, a crowd of villagers, shouting 'We want our old road. Long live the Third Estate!', demolished the wall that Henri Bertin had recently constructed around his new château of Chatou in the canton of Saint-Germain-en-Laye, situated about 40 kilometres west of Paris. It represented a minor episode of the Great Fear that swept through France that famous spring. The villagers, who had drawn up their *cahier des doléances* (books of grievances) just a few months earlier, were righting a perceived wrong—the construction of a new wall and road that would disrupt communication between the peasants of Chatou and their markets in Paris. A year or so later, Henri Bertin would emigrate to Spa in Belgium, where he would die on 16 September 1792, just over a week before the proclamation of the First French Republic.[63]

It was a sad end to Bertin and Moreau's lengthy campaign in favour of a reconstructed Bourbon monarchy. Had they let down their king by insisting on the preservation of absolute monarchy, or had a weak king, surrounded by an antiquated posse of princes and peers, let them down by refusing to settle for a constitutional monarchy? The answer is complicated: Henri Bertin's career should remind us that not all royal ministers were un-Enlightened blockheads, but it is true that Louis XVI (who dismissed Bertin in 1780) recruited more of the old aristocratic guard after 1774 than common sense and circumstance warranted. The consequences of their political ignorance were quite extraordinary. The conservative élite that had seized power in 1789, with the assistance of the popular masses, was fatally fractured after a couple of years by a combination of war, aristocratic reaction, and continuing popular rebellion, especially in the countryside. There is a remarkable resemblance between our analysis of Bertin and Moreau's prospectus for a new élite, and Michael Mann's analysis of French politics 1790–91. Mann argues that the Revolution 'was led by the ideological [monarchist] élite with substantial bourgeois and petit bourgeois backing. The new legitimating principle was the "people" or the "nation"'.[64] It was the scale of popular resistance coupled with the decision to arm the nation against its internal and external enemies that would precipitate the collapse of this new élite and the creation of the Jacobin Terror by 1793.

We would not disagree with Peter Campbell's assertion that 'a fuller comprehension of the traditional forms and structures of political life is extremely important for an understanding of the political crisis in the 1780s', but too many historians have underestimated the severity of the 'social question' by shrinking the length of the 'Pre-Revolution' to a couple of years.[65] Despite the leading political role and class cohesion of the bourgeoisie, it was the popular movement, in town and country, which would dictate the course of the Revolution from 1789 to 1794. It was the peasantry that would secure, first the theoretical 'abolition of feudalism' in August 1789, then its actual abolition by 1794. These were the years which accelerated the process of class formation: 'the Revolution was accomplished, above all, thanks to the efforts of the popular masses in town and country, under the hegemony of the bourgeoisie it is true, but also in the course of the struggle against the bourgeoisie...'[66]

Finally, we should recognise that many Catholic Royalists, such as Bertin and Moreau, also contributed to the creation of the conservative élite that presided over the early years of the Revolution. Despite their fealty to their monarchs, both men recognised the importance of the socio-economic forces that had transformed the old, corporate institutions of French society; they recognised that a 'feudal nobility' was an anachronism, but they also recognised the threat posed by the property-less masses during a period in which 'public opinion' had altered the rules of political engagement. Bertin realised, too late, that it had not been possible to decouple the monarchy and the old nobility. In his last letter to Amiot, Bertin commented on the 'disasters that have befallen France, it was a victim of its own vices, it is collapsing like the Roman Empire under the last Emperors, too heavily burdened by its own faults and corruption'. He closed the letter with a request for a copy of *Confucius et sa morale*.[67] David Parker ends his study of *Class and State in Ancien Régime France* with the comment that 'many nobles, office-holders, merchants and clergy, alike espoused a set of assumptions, largely derived from England, which were fundamentally bourgeois'.[68] In Henri Bertin's case, some of his ideas were drawn from countries as far away as China. It was a 'global enlightenment', perhaps, that helped him to make his personal contribution to the 'rise of the bourgeoisie'?

Notes

1. Throughout this essay, I shall employ the term 'Orthodox' to describe those historians who avowedly adopt a Marxist, or Marxist–Leninist, interpretation of history; the term 'Revisionist' will be used to describe those who specifically seek to challenge the basic premises of the 'Orthodox tradition'.
2. For two informative accounts, see David Parker, *Class and State in Ancien Régime France. The Road to Modernity?* (London, 1996), ch.2, and Peter Jones, *Reform and Revolution in France: The Politics of Transition, 1774–1791* (Cambridge, 1995), ch.3.
3. Bailey Stone, *The Genesis of the French Revolution: a Global-Historical Interpretation* (Cambridge, 1994), p.5.
4. Alfred Cobban, *The Social Interpretation of the French Revolution*, 2nd edn (Cambridge, 1999), pp.xiii–xlviii.
5. See the collection of articles in *The Transition from Feudalism to Capitalism,* introduction by Rodney Hilton (London, 1978).
6. Cobban, *Social Interpretation*, p.32.
7. Cobban, *Social Interpretation*, pp.xxx–xxii.
8. George Taylor, 'The Paris bourse on the eve of the Revolution, 1781–1789', *American Historical Review*, 67 (1962), pp.976–7.
9. William Doyle, 'The Price of Offices in Pre-Revolutionary France', *Historical Journal*, 27 (1984), pp.831–60; Cobban, *The Social Interpretation*, p.xxxviii.
10. Cobban, *The Social Interpretation*, p.107.
11. Cobban, *The Social Interpretation*, p.xxii.
12. Christopher Read, *Lenin* (London, 2005), pp.193–5; Anatoli Ado, 'Le mouvement paysan et le problème de l'égalité, 1789–94', in Albert Soboul (ed.) *Contributions à l'histoire paysanne de la Révolution française* (Paris, 1977).
13. Cobban, *The Social Interpretation*, p.4.
14. Cobban, *The Social Interpretation*, p.126.
15. George Taylor, 'Non-Capitalist Wealth and the Origins of the French Revolution', *American Historical Review*, 72 (1966–7), p.491.
16. There are several, recent collections of articles that bear witness to the longevity and intensity of the debate between Orthodox and Revisionist scholars. For example, Gary Kates (ed.), *The French Revolution: Recent Debates and New Controversies* (London, 1998); Ronald Schechter (ed.), *The French Revolution* (Blackwell, 2001); Peter Campbell (ed.), *The Origins of the French Revolution: Problems in Focus* (Basingstoke, 2006).
17. François Furet, 'Transformations in Historiography', in Ferenc Fehér (ed.), *The Birth of Modernity* (Berkeley, 1990), p.272. For constructive critiques of Furet and

Baker see Peter Campbell's introduction to *The Origins of the French Revolution*, pp.8–9, and Marisa Linton, 'The Intellectual Origins of the French Revolution', pp.152–6; William Scott, 'From Social to Cultural History', pp.117–19.
18. Keith Baker, *The French Revolution and the Creation of Modern Political Culture, Vol. 1: The Political Culture of the Old Regime* (Oxford, 1987), p.xii.
19. Cobban, *The Social Interpretation*, p.16; Furet, 'Transformations in Historiography', p.272.
20. Cobban, *The Social Interpretation*, p.54; Furet, *Marx and the French Revolution* (London, 1988), p.15.
21. Furet, *Marx and the French Revolution*, pp.14, 166.
22. Read, *Lenin*, p.207.
23. Cobban, *The Social Interpretation*, p.xlvi; Furet, 'Transformations in Historiography', pp.268–9.
24. Furet, 'Tranformations in Historiography', p.268.
25. Sara Maza, 'Luxury, Morality and Social Change', in Schechter, *The French Revolution*, pp.178–209.
26. B.N., *Mémoires, mss., relatifs aux privilèges des bourgeois de Périgord, Collection Périgord*, vol.180; Colin Jones, 'The Great Chain of Buying: Medical Advertisement, the Bourgeois Public Sphere, and the Origins of the French Revolution', in Schechter (ed.), *The French Revolution*, pp.141–74.
27. Benoît Garnot, *Le Peuple au siècle des Lumières* (Paris, 1990), p.79; Lewis, *France, 1715–1804* (London, 2004), pp.116–17.
28. Guy Chaussinand-Nogaret, *Choiseul, Naissance de la Gauche* (Paris, 1998).
29. Darrin McMahon, *Enemies of the Enlightenment. The French Counter-Enlightenment and the Making of Modernity* (Oxford, 2001), pp.21, 53, 202–3.
30. Nigel Aston, *Religion and Revolution in France, 1780–1804* (London, 2000), p.3; Dale Van Kley, 'The Religious Origins of the French Revolution, 1560–1791' in Campbell (ed.), *The Origins of the French Revolution*, p.176; David Garrioch, *The Formation of the Parisian bourgeoisie, 1690–1830* (Cambridge, 1996), pp.276–9.
31. *Correspondence des RR.PP, jésuites missionnaires en Chine, avec H-L-J-B Bertin, 1744–98* (hereafter *C.L.*), H. Cordier (ed.), 12 vols, *Bibliothèque de l'Institut de France*.
32. See Gwynne Lewis, 'Henri-Léonard Bertin and the Fate of the Bourbon Monarchy: the Chinese Connection', in *Enlightenment and Revolution: Essays in Honour of Norman Hampson* (Burlington, VT, 2004).
33. *C.L.*, Bertin to abbé Bourgeois, 15 Dec. 1779.
34. Louis Dermigny, *La Chine et l'Occident: le commerce à Canton au XVIIIe siècle*, 3 vols (Paris, 1964), vol.1, p.89.
35. Lewis, 'Henri-Léonard Bertin', p.86.
36. Edmond Dziembowski, *Gabriel-François Coyer, Jacob-Nicolas Moreau: Ecrits sur le patriotisme, l'esprit public et la propagande au milieu du XVIIIe siècle* (La Rochelle, 1997), pp.11–12.
37. Dieter Gembicki, *Histoire et politique à la fin de l'ancien Régime: Jacob-Nicolas Moreau, 1717–1803*, (Paris, Nizet, 1979), p.180.
38. Marx, 'Moralizing Criticism and Critical Morality' in Furet, *Marx and the French*

Revolution, p.177.
39. Daniel Dessert, *Argent, pouvoir et société au grand siècle* (Paris, Fayard, 1984), p.429.
40. Dziembowski, *Gabriel-François Coyer*, p.40.
41. Dziembowski, *Gabriel-François Coyer*, pp.36–7.
42. *C.L.*, Yang to Bertin, 29 Dec. 1767.
43. Gembicki, *Histoire et politique*, p.56.
44. David Garrioch, *Neighbourhood and Community in Paris, 1740–60* (Cambridge, 1986), p.76.
45. Marisa Linton, 'The Intellectual Origins', p.158.
46. Keith Baker, 'Controlling French history: the ideological arsenal of Jacob-Nicolas Moreau', in Keith Baker, *The French Revolution* (Cambridge, 1990), pp.84–5.
47. *C.L.*, Bertin to Amiot, 21 Oct. 1786.
48. Aston, *Religion and Revolution*, pp.96–8.
49. *C.L.*, Ko to Bertin, 5 Oct. 1770; Amiot to Bertin, 28 Sept.1778, and 24 Oct. 1784.
50. *C.L.*, Amiot to Bertin, 15 Nov. 1784.
51. *C.L.*, Bertin to Amiot, 29 Jan. 1790.
52. Munro Price, 'The Court Nobility and the Origins of the Revolution' in Hamish Scott and Brendan Simms (eds), *Cultures of Power in Europe during the Long Eighteenth Century* (Cambridge, 2007), p.287.
53. Lewis, *France, 1715–1804*, ch.5; Benoît Garnot, *Le people au siècle des Lumières* (Paris, 1990), p.44.
54. Jonathan Israel, *Radical Enlightenment: Philosophy and the Making of Modernity, 1650–1750* (Oxford, 2001), p.138.
55. Gembicki, *Histoire et politique*, p.282.
56. John Markoff, *The Abolition of Feudalism* (Pennsylvania, 1996), p.265.
57. Jean Nicolas, *La Rébellion Française: Mouvements populaires et conscience sociale, 1661–1789* (Paris, 2002), p.19–36. See also, Anatoli Ado, *Paysans en Révolution: terre, pouvoir et jacquerie, 1789–94* (Paris, 1996), pp.64–93.
58. Nicolas, *La Rébellion Française*, pp.378–9. See also Robert Schwartz, *The Policing of the Poor in Eighteenth-Century France* (London, 1988), ch.8.
59. Lewis, *France, 1715–1804*, p.183.
60. *The German Ideology*, in Furet, *Marx and the French Revolution*, p.158.
61. Pierre Foncin, *Essai sur le ministère de Turgot* (Paris, 1976), pp.228–30.
62. Nicolas, *La Rébellion Française*, p.538.
63. *B.N., Vivre à Chatou à la fin du XVIIIe siècle: le village retrouvé* (Paris, 1989).
64. Michael Mann, *The Sources of Social Power*, vol.2, *The Rise of Classes and Nation-States, 1760–1914* (Cambridge, 1993).
65. Campbell, *Power and Politics*, p.315.
66. Ado, *Paysans en Révolution*, p.11.
67. *C.L.*, Bertin to Amiot, 29 January 1790.
68. Parker, *Class and State*, p.280.

The Absolutist State of Eighteenth-Century France
Modern Bureaucracy or Feudal Bricolage?

Stephen Miller

Colin Jones's recent work, *The Great Nation: France from Louis XV to Napoleon*, is the first Penguin history of the period to appear in about forty years. As such, it draws on the accumulated research to establish the latest scholarly consensus and the basic text for the general reader. The overall argument is that the bourgeoisie grew in numbers and wealth as a result of commercial capitalism and no longer fit into the self-regulating corporative groups—the clergy, the nobility, provincial estates, associations of judges, notaries, etc.—constitutive of the Bourbon polity. Members of the bourgeoisie instead came to see themselves as citizens of a national community and took the revolutionary step of demanding the corresponding sovereign rights.[1]

Jones maintains that the administrative bureaucracy, established in the second half of the seventeenth century, encouraged rationality and economic growth, and contributed to the rise of the bourgeoisie. Louis XIV, Jones writes, kept the high nobles away from the levers of power and developed policy instead with trained teams of ministers. Louis XIV appointed the members of the ministerial families to the revocable posts of provincial intendant, which unlike the tens of thousands of venal offices did not require a payment to the royal treasury and did not grant the incumbent property rights over his functions. Jones states that the crown turned the intendants into bureaucratic channels for controlling the lineage nobles and associations of venal officers. The opposition of these traditional authorities reinforced the intendants' sense of cohesion with the administrators in Versailles. Together, the royal ministers and intendants upheld standards of hygiene, rationalised government agencies and services, promoted manufacturing and rural development, established agricultural societies and veterinary schools, and succeeded in maintaining order far more effectively than had the administrative structures prior to Louis XIV in the first half of the seventeenth century.[2]

In 1747, Jones writes, the *ponts-et-chaussée* (the department of engineering and public works) founded a school for scientific research and professional training and imparted to its graduates a sense of common purpose and responsibility for the general interest of society. Members of the *ponts-et-chaussée* gained their posts through competitive exams, took inspiration from the enlightenment spirit of reason, and represented a model of military discipline. The *ponts-et-chaussée* generated 'an ethic of loyal state service which prized the values of exchange in unlocking productive resources and stimulating social improvement.'[3] Jones asserts that the monarchy used the *ponts-et-chaussée* to build the best network of major roads in Europe.[4]

Jones grants that Louis XIV offered the nobility the opportunity to retain its rank at the head of the state by attending the royal court, submitting to administrative discipline, and serving in the military and government. Jones offers incisive accounts of essential reforms gone awry because of the meddling of noble clans of the royal court in policy matters. He writes that the monarchy functioned through networks of clients rather than through bureaucratic channels, and that it reordered traditional corporate groups and integrated them closely to the state rather than corrode their privileges. He asserts that foreign mercenaries made up 25 per cent of the royal armies and that recruiting sergeants rounded up village outcasts rather than apply uniform standards of conscription. But on the whole, Jones argues that regarding the century prior to the Revolution as an 'old regime' has led historians to disregard the signs of vitality, to see a political system perceived as strong by its adversaries as decrepit, and to draw mistaken contrasts between the eighteenth-century state and the political changes of the Revolution. The monarchy was animated by '...a renovating technocratic spirit...which sought to rationalise and revivify government services, so that the state could strengthen the country's infrastructure and stimulate the economy.'[5]

Reformist State Independent of Civil Society

There is something to be said for this depiction of the monarchy as a vehicle of progress above the sectional interests of the nobility. For one thing, the king appointed many revocable government agents over the course of the eighteenth century. The intendant of the Lyonnais, for instance, had five sub-delegates under his orders at the beginning of the eighteenth century and nineteen in 1789. The monarchy established schools in Orleans, Amiens, and Metz in the 1770s to train agents for the assessment of *vingtièmes* taxes on all proprietors, including the nobles. It sent hundreds of these fiscal agents to the provinces to investigate inheritances and property transfers and oblige the nobles to pay their proportion of the tax. Such investigations of property transfers could raise the taxes of nobles to over 10 per cent of their landed income.[6]

The monarchy taxed its non-revocable venal officers by withholding a percentage of the annual emoluments it paid to them in recognition for the capital invested in royal service. Moreover, the monarchy constantly squeezed venal officers by threatening to sell duplicate posts, glut the market, and bring down the value of all of them. The office holders would buy up the new creations to protect the value of their professions, and would assimilate the emoluments and privileges of the new creations to their original offices. The problem was that the new emoluments and privileges sometimes did not amount to the market rate of interest. This sort of financial manipulation eroded the wealth and status of the noble judges of the parlements, the fifteen high courts of the realm, at the end of the seventeenth and the first decades of the eighteenth centuries. Offices, which had once formed a capital stock of income, power, and prestige, became instead sources of distress and unease.[7]

Some historians argue that in the decades after 1760, the monarchy developed innovative policies to promote the general interests of society. The monarchy sought to stimulate the economy by freeing labour from the control of the guilds and lifting regulations from the grain trade. It initiated reforms to streamline the financial administration by divesting itself of the venal officers who gathered royal revenue into their private treasuries and gained millions every year at the expense of the king and the taxpayers. Most importantly, the crown held out the promise of putting an end to royal absolutism by inviting royal subjects to participate in provincial assemblies, municipal administrations, and village councils.[8]

Some historians make the case that these reforms amounted to much of the programme carried out by the National Assembly in the first three years of the Revolution. Michel Antoine asserts that the monarchy took progressive steps toward establishing a modern state of law and gaining acceptance of its right to collect a national source of revenue from all proprietors in a verifiable way. While most historians argue that the monarchy did not make so much progress in implementing the reforms, they nonetheless believe that the attempts to do so created awareness in royal subjects of a national community with common interests and a common destiny. Keith Baker and David Bell, in particular, argue that the efforts of royal ministers to alter the governmental practices of the old regime—especially the suppression of the parlements under the chancellor Maupeou in 1771—made manifest the transience of the traditional corporative groups and the dangers of despotic power, and led writers to formulate innovative ways of constituting the state.[9] The proposition is that the revolutionary impulse did not result from inequalities within the government and society of the old regime, but from new modes of thinking about government and society instilled by the administrative initiatives of the crown.

Old Practices and New Challenges

Any evaluation of the role of the state in the development of modern France must contend with evidence that the monarchy did not evolve into a coherent bureaucracy or an efficient administration. This evidence demonstrates overwhelmingly that the monarchy built up the state, not by diminishing the rights of the nobility, but by upholding these rights and gaining the nobility's loyalty. The monarchy enforced a political and juridical context inherited from the middle ages which permitted the nobles to govern in the name of the king and benefit from the economy. The kings, of course, had to contend with a growing population in peasant villages and had to wage ever more costly wars. In seeking to address these challenges, the kings and their ministers often borrowed policy ideas from the feudal past. When they tried to implement original reforms, they faced intractable opposition from the governmental structures of the monarchy.[10]

The department of the *ponts-et-chaussée* provides a perfect example of the monarchy's use of old practices to meet new challenges in a manner acceptable to the nobility. After the founding of the *ponts-et-chaussée* in 1716, the intendants began to furnish its engineers with unpaid labour from rural communities for roadwork. The idea of coercing the peasantry came from the labour services known as the *corvée* due to the feudal lords of the medieval period. Whereas noble and bourgeois proprietors enjoyed exemptions from the royal *corvée* on the roads, the inhabitants of rural communities bore a collective responsibility and could not purchase any sort of discharge. Although the royal *corvée* amounted to only twelve days a year in the Lyonnais, it amounted to far more days in other provinces such as Poitou, where some peasants had to spend sixty days a year labouring on the roads.[11]

The unproductiveness of forced labour became apparent to many observers of the period. The authorities of the *généralité* of Lyon, for instance, contended with so much opposition that by the end of the 1770s, they could no longer force the peasants to labour on the roads no matter how many troops and imprisonments they imposed. Royal reformers argued that a money tax to pay for hired workers would make the work more reliable. The monarchy actually succeeded in setting up a provincial assembly in the Berry and in working with the assembly to abolish the *corvée* on the roads in 1781. The assembly, composed of the élite nobles and jurists of the Berry, augmented the tax on commoners (*taille*) and used the additional funds to hire workers and improve the province's communications.[12]

Elsewhere, the noble magistrates of the judiciary thwarted attempts to replace the *corvée* with a productive system for roadwork. In 1776, the royal minister Turgot proposed legislation for a money tax to finance roadwork. He made the case that the nobles, as large landowners with marketable stocks of produce, benefited the most from the roads and should help pay for their confection. Yet he failed to overcome the resistance of the parlement of Paris, and the tax never saw the light of day. A new attempt to use the provincial assemblies, established in many of the core provinces of the realm in 1787, to convert the *corvée* into a tax for roadwork ran into the opposition of nobles and office holders. In Upper Normandy, municipal officers, local judges, and the parlement of Rouen all opposed the addition of the new tax to the rolls of the capitation to which nobles were liable. They argued that this mode of taxation would swell the coffers of the crown's fiscal receivers rather than raise funds for roadwork. The Norman magistrates prevented collection, and the contractors for roadwork had to suspend operations.[13]

Taxation and Nobility

Royal taxation, like roadwork, generally spared the privileged orders. In theory, nobles had to pay the *taille* on the land they managed directly when it exceeded the area of four ploughings. Tenants paid the *taille* on the land they rented from nobles and thus presumably did not pay as much rent as they otherwise could have. While there is debate about how much of the *taille* the nobles paid from farms exceeding four ploughings and from the reduction of land rents caused by their tenants' tax payments, the documents on the allotment of the *taille* show that the nobles foisted a disproportionate share on the poorest and weakest peasants. Many rural communities sent memorandums to the provincial assembly of Poitou in 1788 stating that needy residents bore an excessive share of tax quotas, because many of the collectors served the local seigneurs, clergymen and privileged proprietors as stewards and treated them favorably in the allotment of the *taille*. Day labourers and other village residents wrote dozens of letters to the provincial assembly of the Berry in the 1780s complaining that the collectors shifted the burden of the taille onto the peasants of modest means to avoid antagonising the affluent proprietors and tenant farmers of the seigneurs.[14]

Furthermore, office holders, clergymen, and nobles usually had properties scattered across several communities and had the right to subsume all of the assessments into one lump payment. It was generally recognised in the 1770s and 1780s that this privilege of the *transport des cotes* permitted large landowners to undervalue their properties or even omit some of the assessments entirely. One of the tasks of the provincial assemblies set up in 1787 was to make the taille more equitable, and the assemblies of Upper Normandy and the Lyonnais sought to end the *transport des cotes*. But the noble magistrates of the *cours des aides* of Paris and Rouen, high courts with jurisdiction over fiscal litigation, refused to authorise changes to the practice and even succeeded in having the king make debate of the issue illegal.[15]

In 1695 Louis XIV promulgated a new tax known as the capitation on all residents of the realm, including the privileged orders, to surmount the inadequacies of the taille. The capitation did not lead to opposition, in part because it was based on a schedule of social ranks and retained all of the monarchy's hierarchies in its assessment. In the eighteenth century, as the capitation became a standard part of the fiscal system, the monarchy made nearly 95 per cent of it an accessory to the rolls of the taille on commoners, even though these taxpayers owned less than 50 per cent of the land in most parts of the kingdom.[16]

The monarchy introduced the *dixième* in 1710 to tax the land values of all proprietors regardless of their social rank. Many nobles, however, refused to declare their wealth, and the tax raised only 24 million *livres* in good years, whereas royal ministers had hoped for 120 million. The intendant of Limoges estimated that three quarters of the province's proprietors failed to declare their wealth and that the rest made fraudulent declarations. Opposition to the *dixième* led the crown to revoke most of its provisions after Louis XIV's death in 1715.[17]

Royal ministers revived this universal tax to offset the costs of wars in the middle of the eighteenth century. The Estates of Languedoc—which, along with the Estates of Brittany, Burgundy and other lesser provinces on the periphery of the realm collectively known as the *pays d'état*, were the only medieval assemblies of the clergy, the nobility, and town leaders to survive into the eighteenth century—opposed the monarchy's plan to impose the tax (at this point called the *vingtième*) on land formerly exempt. The crown then suspended the right of Languedoc's bishops, barons, and town oligarchs to hold their annual estates and began assessing the *vingtième* through royal agents. But the paucity of royal personnel and the urgent need for revenue, as war with England and Prussia loomed on the horizon, led Louis XV to reconvene the Estates and allow them to administer the tax in return for annual payments to the royal treasury. In Burgundy, the crown initially insisted on assessing the *vingtième* through royal commissioners but then agreed in 1756 to allow the Estates to administer the tax in return for annual payments to the royal treasury. The Estates of Burgundy then consented to further *vingtièmes* in 1760 and 1782, once the crown abandoned its intent to verify incomes and collect the taxes. In this manner, the nobles prevented the *vingtièmes* from systematically taxing their income.[18]

In the core provinces of the realm bereft of estates, (the *pays d'élections*), the monarchy sought to levy a new *vingtième* tax in 1763 in order to overcome the debt crisis caused by royal borrowing during the Seven Years War; this *vingtième* was to be of unlimited duration and based on an official register of the ownership, extent, and value of real property. Several of the parlements refused to accept the plan and hindered the efforts of the royal intendants and military governors to forcibly apply it. The judges incited opposition to taxation along the royal chain of command, and the fiscal system ground to a halt in many parts of the country. The king had to limit the duration of the *vingtième* and renounce his intent to investigate landed wealth in order to regain the cooperation of the high courts and maintain control of the provinces.[19]

In dire financial straits in 1787, the monarchy convoked the potentates of the first two estates to an Assembly of Notables to endorse a territorial subvention equal for all proprietors regardless of their status. The Assembly objected that the territorial subvention would take productive resources from proprietors and harm agriculture. The members declared their own incompetence to deliberate on such a fundamental change of the laws of the realm and refused to approve the new tax.[20]

Unable to impose the territorial subvention, the monarchy nonetheless secured the consent of the parlement of Paris to investigations of landed revenue with the purpose of augmenting the *vingtièmes*. The king immediately invited the newly established provincial assemblies, composed of clergymen, nobles, and jurists selected by the king and his advisors among the foremost provincial families, to take responsibility for collection and grant the king annual payments. These were to be based on the anticipated increase in revenue once land incomes had been properly assessed. The provincial assemblies, however, claimed that the investigations would not increase the *vingtièmes* and that the tax burden should actually be reduced.[21]

In Provence—a province under a unique administration, the *assemblée générale des communautés*, bringing together the privileged élites of a handful of towns—the crown upheld a system of *taille réelle*, prevalent in southern

France, in which certain lands rather than privileged orders bore tax-exemptions. A royal declaration of 1666 stipulated that once nobles sold their tax-exempt land it forever lost its privileges. Subsequent land transactions may have diminished the nobility's exemptions. Cases came up in the 1770s and 1780s in which nobles sought to recover their privileges by asserting seigneurial rights over their vassals' lands and integrating the lands into their tax-exempt holdings. But the crown took the side of the *assemblée générale des communautés* and helped it to expand the fiscal capacity of the Provençal countryside by protecting the tax-paying lands of the communities. Rather than consent to the loss of their privileges, the nobles revived the Estates of Provence in 1787, established their authority over the *assemblée générale des communautés*, and set about the reconstitution of their exemptions. In Provence, as elsewhere in the realm, the only perceptible outcome of the crown's efforts to levy taxes on the nobility was the crystallisation of public opinion against arbitrary government. Nobles, office holders and municipal élites came to believe that 'the nation' had the right to debate taxation and allocate public revenues through the representatives of the three orders in provincial and national estates.[22]

Feudal Precedents

The king and the nobles of the royal court collected feudal forms of rent in addition to the taxes on the land. Early in the seventeenth century, the crown began to assert its right of universal *domaine direct*, that all fiefs ultimately belonged to the king and that he had the right to collect revenue from them. The king revived his feudal claims in order to obtain income selling exemptions to the nobles and large proprietors threatened by his seigneural rights. The crown continued to collect seigneurial payments from the holders of fiefs into the second half of the eighteenth century.[23]

The king also used his feudal prerogatives on behalf of the high-ranking nobles of Versailles. Louis XVI granted an *apanage* or fief of the province of Poitou to his brother, the comtet d'Artois, in 1778 in exchange for some of the count's seigneurial holdings elsewhere in the country. Poitevin communities and lords complained that the efforts of Artois's office holders to augment his revenues obliged them to make periodic payments and encroached upon their income from provincial woods. Another one of the king's brothers, the duc d'Orléans, enjoyed annual revenue of seven million *livres*, perhaps the highest income in the realm, over half of which derived from an *apanage* given by the king. Two thirds of the revenue of Orléans's fief came from land rents, the rest from seigneurial dues.[24]

The crown appointed many of the first military governors in the fourteenth and fifteenth centuries to maintain order in the regions acquired from formerly autonomous counts and dukes. The governorships served as rewards for the feudal magnates who fought on the king's side in wars. By the end of the sixteenth century, the governorships developed into hereditary political property, and like other feudal jurisdictions, were sold on the market or passed on to heirs with all of their influence, honors and revenues. The king's appointment of intendants to the provinces at the end of the sixteenth century did not reduce the power of the governors but rather rendered them more effective by demonstrating to provincial subjects that the laws of the realm, certified by the king's commissioners, required obedience to the governors and the levies they enforced. The governors tended to reside in the capital and serve as intermediaries for urban élites to advance their interests with the king. Provincial estates and municipalities disbursed ever larger pensions to stay in the good graces of the governors and benefit from their influence with the king. The princes of Condé, hereditary governors of Burgundy and prime collaborators of the crown, remained closely involved in the administration of the province from their residence in Chantilly just north of Paris. The princes helped select the intendants of Burgundy, named the officers of the Estates, and stage-managed the triennial meetings during the entire last century of the old regime.[25]

The ducs de Villeroy, residents of Versailles and members of the king's councils, held the title of hereditary governors of Lyon and had seigneurial jurisdiction over the city, the second of France, during the seventeenth and eighteenth centuries. The municipal government, or consulat, consisting of the provost marshal of the merchants and aldermen, wrote to the dukes at least four times a week. This correspondence with a feudal overlord, rather than standard bureaucratic channels, remained the means by which the consulat made requests to the central government. The consulat made periodic gifts and payments to the Villeroys for advancing its interests. In return for looking after Lyon's élite, the Villeroys retained the power to arrange for the election of their favorites at the biannual renewal of the provost marshal of the merchants and aldermen. These officials then passed before the Villeroys in a ceremonial reception before taking up their duties.[26]

In 1765, the king granted seigneurial rights over the nearby town of Saint-Etienne to François Peirenc de Moras, seigneur de Saint-Priest, royal minister and former secretary of state. Henceforth, the litigation and with it the legal fees of thousands of urban residents flowed through de Moras's tribunal. The municipal nobility, bourgeoisie, and religious confraternities were quick and vigorous to challenge their subjection to de Moras's seigneurial jurisdiction, but the parlement of Paris decided the case in his favour. The king bestowed this jurisdiction in 1776 on Pierre Gilbert de Voisins, president in the parlement of Paris and key member of the royal ministry. For over three decades from 1765 until the Revolution, Saint-Etienne lacked a town government and bourgeois militia to maintain order, because the local élites refused to serve under a distant seigneur who appointed his own officers to the municipal tax farms and administration.[27]

These examples suggest that the kings and high-ranking nobles of the royal court used feudal precedents to the disadvantage of nobles and landowners in the provinces. But upon closer examination, one sees that the crown sustained the relevance of medieval laws advantageous to these élites. The kings played the role of pre-eminent lords of a country seeped in feudal tradition. They showed by example that seigneurial titles could be exploited for economic gain. Scholarly studies of various regions demonstrate that the seigneurial classes employed jurists to analyze their old feudal documents, find abeyant rights and dues to impose on peasant communities, and augment their landed income in the second half of the eighteenth century.[28]

Crown and Provincial Élites

Many intendants sought to improve the administration and economy of their provinces. Their first task, however, to maintain order, required them to uphold the laws on the registers of the parlements, the *cours des aides*, and the plethora of lesser tribunals. In addition to the decrees and ordinances of the king, the laws included provincial customs and an accumulation of jurisprudence all of which was permeated by feudal concepts and assumptions and none of which significantly undermined seigneurial prerogatives. If the intendants moved against the magistrates and seigneurs, they risked public opposition and unrest. The intendants often found it useful to adopt the contrary course of working within the laws and in alliance with the traditional authorities to accomplish royal goals. The tendency of the king and his intendants to work with the magistrates and seigneurs, notwithstanding the tensions between the central and local authorities, indicates the limits imposed on the crown by the presence of a readily identifiable ruling class from which in any case the intendants were drawn.[29]

William Beik's study of seventeenth-century Languedoc is the best statement of this understanding of absolutism as an alliance between the crown and the provincial élites. Beik shows that Louis XIV worked with the nobles in the tribunals and the Estates of Languedoc to maintain order and collect taxes and that this arrangement permitted the nobles to reap the benefits of the provincial economy. While the eighteenth century saw changes in the economic, intellectual, and financial context of Languedoc, the authorities confronting these changes remained essentially the same as those of the seventeenth century studied by Beik. Distinguished nobles, appointed by the king to the province's twenty-three bishoprics, gained enormous annual revenues of between 30,000 and 500,000 *livres* from these ecclesiastical benefices. The bishops formed the entire first order of the Estates of Languedoc and—together with the second order, composed of twenty-three barons of long lineage, and the third order, composed of seventy-three oligarchs of the towns (often nobles chosen by bishops and seigneurs)—managed the province's finances, supervised the lodging of royal troops, and saw to the construction and maintenance of the roads. The noble magistrates of the *Cour des Comptes, Aides et Finances* of Montpellier and the parlement of Toulouse owned the largest domains in the hinterlands of the provincial capitals, had rights to influential posts in the municipal councils, and arbitrated thousands of disputes every year through their offices at the head of the Languedocien judiciary. Moreover, most of these élites acquired a portion of Languedoc's fiscal revenue through offices in the tax farms, emoluments distributed at the meetings of the Estates, and investments in the debts of the Estates and the subordinate administrative bodies.[30]

One finds much the same story in Burgundy and Brittany. The Estates of Burgundy brought together 66 abbeys, bishops, and priors, nobles of long lineage (about 75 at a typical meetings), and 25 mayors of the towns every three years. The Estates of Brittany annually brought together bishops, abbeys, and the deputies of the cathedral chapter, all of the provincial nobles (between 357 and 855 attended), and the oligarchs of the towns, including many urban nobles. The Estates of Burgundy and Brittany regulated markets, saw to the construction and maintenance of the roads, controlled provincial finances, and preserved a moderate tax burden for the local landowners. From the king's perspective, the fiscal yields may have been relatively low but were also sufficiently stable for the Estates to service loans for the royal treasury. The crown had ready sources of cash, while the provincial landowners had opportunities to invest in bonds yielding reliable returns of 5 per cent. The officials of the Estates of Burgundy, such as the secretaries who kept the Condés abreast of provincial affairs, and the magistrates of the chamber of accounts who audited the financial records, collected ample rewards for their services. The tax farm run by the Estates of Brittany provided a vital source of employment and income for hundreds of the province's nobles.[31]

The nobles of the *pays d'élections* did not have the benefit of provincial estates yet secured influential positions in urban institutions. All of the great families of the region of Lyon had members in the local tribunals and municipal government (*consulat*). Indeed, most of the nobles of the Lyonnais obtained their rank between the fifteenth and eighteenth centuries through the purchase of offices and especially through 'election' to the *consulat* as aldermen. The wealthiest ones typically owned a financial office of municipal treasurer or general tax receiver, and added the office to their post of alderman in the town government. Offices in the tax farms and the financial administration furnished the greatest fortunes in Lyon. The dowries and living standards of the nobles far surpassed those of the city's commercial classes. Appositely, given their wealth and status, the nobles of Lyon passed much of their time at their chateaux, seigneuries, and landholdings in the hinterland.[32]

As the social stratification of Lyon suggests, venal offices generally turned out to be lucrative investments. The number of offices had quadrupled between 1515 and 1665, and the share of overall taxation accruing to the purchasers increased by an even greater proportion. Louis XIV taxed offices and reduced their emoluments to raise revenue for his interminable wars of the latter part of his reign. The crown made few financial demands on office holders after his death between the 1720s and 1740s, but again taxed offices and forced loans from their owners to help fund the spiralling costs of wars in the latter part of the 1740s and the decades after 1750. Nevertheless, in spite of the crown's financial demands on office holders, the most thorough studies of the venal system show that offices generally turned out to be lucrative investments. Many office holders succeeded in maintaining emoluments at 5 per cent of the capital value, and others made additional revenue collecting fees from common subjects. In 1788, over 16 per cent of the 821,921 *livres* collected by the monarchy from the commoners of the Berry for the *taille* remained in the province to cover the emoluments of tax-exempt magistrates. When one adds the fees collected from litigants, some venal judgships had annual returns as high as 10 or 12 per cent of their capital value. Financial offices, conferring emoluments, a percentage of the fiscal proceeds, and bonuses to cover administrative costs, offered even better returns. The receivers, treasurers, and tax farmers at the top of the fiscal establishments garnered hundreds of thousands of *livres* a year and formed part of the most prestigious noble circles of the kingdom.[33]

Government posts also conferred political responsibilities. The magistrates of the kingdom's twenty-nine bureaus of finances judged disputes arising out of the alignment of the roads and the king's seigneurial holdings, worked with the intendant to allot taxes among the parishes, and verified and certified the royal fiscal demands before passing them on to the localities. The judges of the parlement of Paris served as the supreme judicial authority over a vast region covering about two thirds of the realm. Every year they made thousands of legal decisions regulating the lives of the populace. The magistrates' role as the guardians of order even led them to assume the administration of the parish churches of Paris in the 1750s and 1760s to ensure that priests offered the sacraments to lay people in the last days of life, including the lay people adhering to the Jansenist interpretation of Catholicism, an anathema to the king and the bishops.[34]

Government posts also conferred the right to display a superior virtue and excellence. Royal officials took the moral direction for their professional activity from the lineage nobles at the top of the social hierarchy who believed that the traditions of the feudal past provided examples of courage and honour for the greatness of France. The nobles, as the bearers of the medieval heritage of the nation, had to enjoy privileges, they held, in order to maintain proper standards for royal subjects. Typical of this outlook were the rulings of the consulat and superior council (set up temporarily between 1771 and 1774 to replace the parlements suppressed by the chancellor Maupeou) of Lyon in 1772, and another ruling of the consulat in 1787, intended to maintain public order by prohibiting commoners from bearing arms. The prohibition did not apply to nobles, the rulings stated, because the prerogatives of high justice of their fiefs included the right to hunt. The nobles and office holders of the magistracy deemed that the seigneurial classes had a historic relationship to the medieval knights and military traditions of the monarchy and should therefore enjoy privileges such as the right to display their weapons in the presence of unarmed common subjects.[35]

It must be acknowledged that the élite clergymen, nobles, venal officers, and municipal authorities sometimes engaged in bitter rivalries and disputes to gain the king's favour and establish their precedence. Some disputes had degenerated into revolts, civil war and popular mobilisations in the first half of the seventeenth century. In the latter part of the eighteenth century, the magistrates of the bureaus of finances paid an agent in Versailles to lobby for their economic interests, defend their jurisdictions against other venal tribunals, and bolster their position relative to other associations in ceremonial receptions, inaugurations, and church services. All of the time, the money, and the anxiety that went into securing the benefits of offices may help explain the paradox that although the propertied classes bid up the price of offices and vigorously defended their jurisdictions and privileges in the last years of the old regime; in the *cahiers de doléances* (books of grievances) and pamphlets sent to Versailles in spring of 1789 they opposed the whole practice of venality on the grounds that it inhibited talent. Some historians look at these rivalries as evidence that the crown divided the élites into orders and prevented them from forming a social class. Clergymen, nobles, and office holders competed for the king's favour in order to enhance their privileges relative to one another rather than to unite as a ruling class to defend their privileges against the rest of the society. Rivalries between the élites permitted the king to maintain absolute power over them.[36]

Then again, unity seems too much to demand of the élites as the qualification for constituting a ruling class. After all, they held fiscal privilege, seigneurial authority and revenue, and the profit, power, and honor of offices over and against the rest of the population. A common programme in defense of their privileges would have been unpopular to say the least. The only programme the seigneurs and office holders could advance was monarchical sovereignty and veneration for the traditional laws of the kingdom. Looked at in this way, the growing number of revocable agents of the crown did not signal the imposition of policy against the interests of the upper clergy and nobility, but rather the improved capacity of the monarchy to settle their rival claims. Between roughly the 1660s and 1770s, élites sent competing grievances in memoranda to Versailles, had the grievances settled in rulings of the king's council, and avoided conflicts liable incite popular involvement in politics. Of course in allowing the king to resolve disputes, power became concentrated in fewer hands. In the eighteenth century, political decisions were made in Versailles and sent out through the intendants, bishops, and leading nobles in the provinces. But by associating themselves with this constellation of power, provincial seigneurs and office holders shared the king's glory and promoted respect for their governmental responsibilities and privileges. In sum, the ruling class required a religiously inspired, glorious and sovereign monarch capable of assuring its various segments a relatively peaceful enjoyment of their privileges *vis-à-vis* one another and the crown, and especially *vis-à-vis* the common subjects of the realm.[37]

Towards Crisis

This system stumbled toward crisis in the second half of the eighteenth century, as costly wars forced the king and his ministers to question the traditional methods of government. The monarchy began to sell venal offices in the sixteenth century to finance military campaigns. But by the time of the Seven Years War between 1756 and 1762, the sale of offices and the payments of their holders raised only 5 per cent of the necessary funds.

Similarly, the networks of financiers, which had traditionally raised loans for the royal treasury against the taxes promulgated by the monarchy during the seventeenth and eighteenth centuries, no longer had the capacity to gather sufficient funds for all of the king's financial commitments. The monarchy had to look elsewhere for credit in the 1780s.[38]

The most common source of credit was the loans raised through the *hôtel de ville* (municipality) of Paris. The king thus borrowed 4,279,715,910 *livres* between 1702 and 1787. The problem with these loans was that the king's poor credit obliged him to pay interest as high as 9 or 10 per cent. These ruinous loans were the immediate cause of the financial crisis that forced the monarchy to call the Estates General in 1788. The monarchy obtained loans on better terms from provincial estates and municipalities. It borrowed about 330,000,000 *livres* from the Estates of Artois, Cambrésis, Flandre, Brittany, Burgundy, and Languedoc at an interest rate of about 5 per cent between 1740 and 1789. These institutions, however, had limited financial capacities. The Estates of Languedoc—which raised a greater volume of loans for the monarchy, over 140 million *livres*, than did any institution outside of the *hôtel de ville* of Paris between 1733 and 1788—teetered on the brink of bankruptcy in last years of the old regime.[39]

The monarchy's efforts to expand the pool of taxable resources and relieve the financial strain on its institutions infringed upon the privileges of rentiers, magistrates and property owners, sometimes provoking recriminations among these élites or uniting them against the crown when it pursued reforms which encroached upon their common interests. The crown took the side of well-to-do commoners and peasant communities against their lords and office holders and disregarded the seigneurial claims to the land inherited from the middle ages in several high-profile court cases in Languedoc, Burgundy, Provence, and the pays d'Auge of Normandy in the 1770s and 1780s. The crown and its commissioners pursued this course in order to broaden the basis of municipal and village councils and encourage wider strata of the population to take an interest in the local administration and economy so that they might improve public services and agricultural lands and ultimately generate more tax revenue for the king.[40]

But in each of these regions, the crown's efforts to solve the fiscal impasse came to naught. Factions of high-ranking nobles advanced their interests at the very heart of the government, and pulled royal policy in contradictory directions. As previously mentioned, the king and the upper circles of the nobility reinforced feudal law by insisting on their seigneurial rights. They thus insured that the efforts of the reformers to limit the scope of seigneurial authority would be episodic and inconsequential. Likewise, the crown's enduring tendency to oblige local authorities to buy up new posts and privileges and protect the value of their governmental responsibilities entrenched the rights of municipal élites to their offices and prerogatives and undermined the efforts of reformers to broaden the basis of local government.[41]

Moreover, the monarchy did not have the bureaucratic capacity to overcome the alliance of seigneurs and venal judges in the provinces. Many of the magistrates of the royal tribunals held lordly rights and enforced customs and jurisprudence inherited from the middle ages. Royal tribunals generally favoured large proprietors in land disputes, defended seigneurial property, and enforced the lords' monopolies over mills, markets, fish ponds, and wine presses. The venal judges of these tribunals were far more numerous than were the reformers in Versailles, and they were better informed of the disputes between lords and peasants. Besides, the judges had wealth and influence in the provinces and often succeeded in resisting policies contrary to their interests. Ultimately, the only concrete result of the efforts of the reformist ministers to limit the authority of seigneurs and office holders in the provinces was to convince many nobles that the monarchy disdained time-honored forms of property and veered toward arbitrary rule.[42]

Royal policy toward the towns raised the same sorts of concerns. The consulat of Lyon took out loans for the king's war effort against England and increased the city's debt from 30 million *livres* in 1775 to 39 million over the next several years. But it had to augment excise taxes to cover the service charges. Popular revolts against the new burdens in 1786 caused panic among urban property owners. The consulat freed detainees from the local prison in an effort to calm the populace and eventually had to call in royal troops to restore order. The political élites of Lille, members by right of the Estates of Walloon Flanders, became quasi royal agents over the course of the eighteenth century. They took out a growing volume of loans and accumulated ever larger debts to satisfy the king's mounting fiscal demands on the city. By the end of the 1780s, Lille's fiscal receipts no longer covered the service charges of the debt despite increases in the excise taxes far above the rate of inflation. In both Lyon and Lille, the inability of the political élites to manage local finances and maintain order led well-to-do residents to publish pamphlets and convene assemblies to demand representation in municipal government in 1787, 1788, and 1789.[43]

Debates

These protests formed part of the first general movement against the old regime. To be sure, the monarchy had contended with rebellious peasants and artisans leery of the possibility of tax increases ever since the first half of the seventeenth century. Royal taxation, especially indirect excises, provoked 466 rebellions between 1661 and 1700, 871 between 1701 and 1730, 794 between 1731 and 1760, and 1,249 between 1761 and 1789. The inhabitants of Auch brandished pikes and disrupted the meetings of the upper clergy, lineage nobles, and jurists of the provincial assembly of Gascony in 1787 when rumors spread that these élites demanded tens of the thousands of *livres* for lavish displays of their attendance. Peasants and artisans knew that the nobility benefited from an inequitable system. They were conscious of class relations but did not conceive of alternatives to monarchical government.[44]

The crown did not permit political discussions liable to lead to such conceptions. Jurists were the only ones with a public forum for debating the affairs of state. The judges, to be sure, rarely availed themselves of this freedom on account of their stake in the system. They generally enforced religious observance, the seigneurial regime, and respect for the crown. Barristers generally upheld the established order, because their distinguished associations constituted integral parts of the royal judiciary. Ambitious lawyers occasionally won public acclaim by pleading in an irreverent manner, flouting the strictures of the judiciary, and by writing inflammatory trial briefs, denouncing their opponents as aristocrats inclined to self-interest and vice.[45]

These were minority voices until the last two years of the old regime, when the financial crisis so debilitated the monarchy that it could no longer stifle public debate. Over the course of the eighteenth century, the Estates of Burgundy gained authority by helping the crown administer the province and raise revenue. The Estates paid for this expanded role in government by appearing to the provincial populace as agents of tyranny and holders of illegitimate privilege. In 1787, well-to-do commoners protested the fiscal immunities of the Burgundian nobility and demanded the right to elect the deputies of the Estates. Well-to-do residents of Languedoc met in scores of assemblies in 1788 and the beginning of 1789 to protest their exclusion from the provincial estates. Dozens of memoranda written in assemblies of the third estate and lower clergy criticised the hold of nobles and bishops on the best posts in the governmental and ecclesiastical hierarchy of Languedoc.[46]

Artisans, merchants, sailors, lawyers, clerks and other members of an assembly of the third estate of Sables d'Olonne in Poitou wrote a memorandum to the king in January 1789 that their professions served the public good but were held in servitude by the clergy and nobility. Members of the first two estates, the assembly pronounced, enjoyed privileges, wealth, and expanses of property, received all sorts of gifts, bonuses, pensions, and honours from the authorities, and refused to lighten the burden on the third estate by sharing the common status of citizen and contributing equally to taxation. Two months later, the general assembly of the third estate, meeting in the provincial capital of Poitiers, prefaced its *cahiers* by stating that the third estate should have as many deputies as the first two combined in the Estates General and that votes should be counted by head rather than by order. This electoral procedure, the assembly contended, would silence prejudices and sentiments of rank. The assembly declared that distinctions and tax exemptions emerged in the time of feudal usurpation and lordly domination, and should be definitively abolished. The assembly stated that commoners should not suffer the stigma of exclusion from any dignity or prerogative reserved for the nobility and clergy. In general, the *cahiers* of the third estate in France as a whole expressed an eagerness to abolish privilege, to see the deputies meet and vote in the Estates General as equals, with as many representatives of the third estate as of the first two combined, and to further the career opportunities of commoners in the military and judiciary.[47]

The nobles, by contrast, did not advance a positive programme liable to win widespread support in the *cahiers* and elections leading up to the Estates General. They recoiled before the idea of an abstract sovereign nation and a uniform code of laws equal for all its members. They saw the nation as an aggregate of orders, each with a special relationship to the king, similar to the vassal's faith in feudal or patrimonial relations of authority. Many assemblies of nobles called for freedom of the press, periodic meetings of the Estates General, and the elimination of trade barriers. Many also agreed to renounce tax exemptions, so long as the nobles could meet as a separate order. The nobles of Bourges stated that their deputies should not transact any business until their ancient rights of assembly, the rights inherent in their lands and persons, be acknowledged. The nobles of Poitiers stated that they would renounce pecuniary privileges, as long as the monarchy maintained its ancient and constitutional forms. These forms meant the conservation of the nobles' rights, prerogatives, distinctions, and properties, 'necessary to the Constitution of the Realm, since, without Nobility, there cannot be Monarchy and since without distinctions and rights to pre-eminence, there cannot be Nobility.' The nobles' tendency to insist on the preservation of distinctions, old institutions, and seigneurial rights rendered their grand renunciations of tax exemptions hollow.[48]

Conclusion

In conclusion, any measure or typology of the modern state—the transformation of the civil servant from proprietor of an office to executor of its duties, the immunity of portions of the state from manipulation by élites, the appointment of civil servants based on proven expertise, the payment of regular salaries to civil servants, a clearly defined hierarchy of offices, uniform abstract laws equal for all, etcetera—shows the fundamentally traditional, even feudal, makeup of the old regime. The royal administration and military upheld a legal system permeated with medieval provisions for burdens on commoners, primarily the peasantry, and titles, exemptions, seigneurial rights, and venal offices for a minority of wealthy subjects, primarily the nobility. International military competition put the monarchy under pressure to reform the government and augment its financial capacity. But nobles, seigneurs, and office holders used their positions within the state to thwart policies counter to their interests.

A proper understanding of the old regime state sheds light on the popular involvement and violence of the Revolution. The privileges of the old regime élites represented burdens to the rest of the population. The king's subjects saw the attachment of the nobles, seigneurs, and office holders to their exclusive rights. After 1789, as France faced the crises of counter-revolution, foreign invasion, and spiraling prices, it proved impossible for the élites to convince the rest of the population that they would take charge of the interests of the country as a whole. Many citizens did not trust the urgent affairs of the nation to those who had long defended privileged private interests. The popular classes harboured suspicions about their erstwhile rulers and took matters into their own hands once the political context offered the occasion.

Notes

1. Colin Jones, *The Great Nation: France from Louis XV to Napoleon* (London, 2003), pp.xxii–xxiv, 166–9, 181–4, 330.
2. Jones, *Great Nation*, pp.9–12, 14–15, 42, 113, 123–4, 155, 169, 256–9.
3. Jones, *Great Nation*, p.256.
4. Jones, *Great Nation*, pp.115, 257.
5. Jones, *Great Nation*, pp.xiv–xv, xx. The quote is on page 256 amid a discussion of the monarchy's efforts to promote economic growth between 1750 and the

early 1780s. For Jones's concessions to the patrimonial view of the state see, pp.15–18, 140–1, 326, 329.
6. Françoise Bayard, 'Les pouvoirs dans la ville,' in Françoise Bayard and Pierre Cayez (eds) *Histoire de Lyon: des origines à nos jours* (Le Coteau, 1990), 2:94; Marcel Marion, *L'impôt sur le revenu au dix-huitième siècle: principalement en Guyenne* (Genève, 1976), pp.223–5; Michael Kwass, *Privilege and the Politics of Taxation in Eighteenth-Century France: Liberté, Égalité, Fiscalité* (Cambridge, 2000), pp.56–7, 95.
7. Kwass, *Privilege and the Politics of Taxation*, pp.105, 204; David Bien, 'Offices, Corps, and a System of State Credit: The Uses of Privilege under the *Ancien Regime*,' in Keith Baker (ed.), *The French Revolution and the Creation of Modern Political Culture* (Oxford, 1987), 1:89–114; John Hurt, *Louis XIV and the Parlements: The Assertion of Royal Authority* (Manchester, 2002), pp.12, 110–11, 116, 183–4, 189.
8. Gail Bossenga, *The Politics of Privilege: Old Regime and Revolution in Lille* (Cambridge, 1991), pp.12–13, 203; J. F. Bosher, *French Finances 1770–1795: From Business to Bureaucracy* (Cambridge, 1970), pp.166, 306–7; Peter Jones, *Reform and Revolution in France: The Politics of Transition, 1774–1791* (Cambridge, 1995), pp.7–9, 114, 141.
9. Jones, *Reform and Revolution in France*, pp.8–9, 60, 120–1, 159, 240; Michel Antoine, 'La Monarchie Absolue,' in *The French Revolution and the Creation of Modern Political Culture*, 1:20; Bossenga, *The Politics of Privilege: Old Regime and Revolution in Lille*, p.40; Keith Baker, 'French Political Thought at the Accession of Louis XVI', *The Journal of Modern History* 50 (1978) p.283; David Bell, *Lawyers and Citizens: The Making of a Political Elite in Old Regime France* (Oxford, 1994), pp.13, 206.
10. Perry Anderson, *Lineages of the Absolutist State* (London, 1974); William Beik 'The Absolutism of Louis XIV as Social Collaboration,' *Past and Present*, 188 (2005), pp.195–224.
11. Abbé L. Chatelard, '*La corvée royale dans le Lyonnais* (1720–1789)', *Revue d'histoire de Lyon* 7 (1908), pp.161, 164–5, 167, Pierre Clément, *La Corvée des chemins en France et spécialement en Poitou sous les intendants de Blossac et Boula de Nanteuil (1751–1790)* (Poitiers, 1899), pp.20, 22–3.
12. Clément, *La Corvée des chemins*, pp.116–18, 122, 145; Chatelard, 'La *corvée* royale dans le Lyonnais,' pp.179, 181, 184–5; Lucien Lachaze, *Les États provinciaux de l'ancienne France et la question des États provinciaux aux XVIIe et XVIIIe siècles: l'assemblée provinciale du Berri sous Louis XVI* (Paris, 1909), pp.129–32, 439.
13. Bailey Stone, *The Parlement of Paris, 1774–1789* (Chapel Hill, 1981), pp.93, 96; Georges Coeuret, *L'assemblée provinciale de Haute-Normandie, 1787–1789* (Paris, 1927), pp.87–8, 138–42.
14. Eugène Louis (ed.), *Le Bas-Poitou en 1788: mémoires addressés à la Commission intermédiaire de l'Assemblée d'élection de Fontenay par les municipalités de Maillezais et de Chaillé-les-Marais* (La Roche-sur-Yon, 1877–1880), pp.5, 10, 43, 45, 256; Archives Départementales du Cher (hereafter ADC), C1114.
15. Coeuret, *L'assemblée provinciale de Haute-Normandie*, 107, 119; *Procès-verbal des*

séances de la première assemblée provinciale de la généralité de Lyon (Lyon, 1787), pp.45–6.
16. ADC 1142: Marcel Marion, *Les impôts directs sous l'ancien régime, principalement au XVIIIe siècle* (Paris, 1910), pp.50–1, 53, 55–8; E. Brossard and Joseph Delapoix de Fréminville, *Histoire du département de la Loire pendant la revolution française (1789–1799)* (Saint-Étienne, 1904–1907), p.77.
17. Richard Bonney, *The Limits of Absolutism in Ancien Régime France* (Aldershot, 1995), pp.401, 405, 409, 412; Peter Campbell, *Power and Politics in Old Regime France, 1720–1745* (London, 1996), p.279.
18. Marcel Marion, *Histoire financière de la France depuis 1715* (New York, 1965), 1:174; Julian Swann, *Provincial Power and Absolute Monarchy: The Estates General of Burgundy, 1661–1790* (Cambridge, 2003), pp.306, 308–9.
19. David Hudson, 'The Parlementary Crisis of 1763', *Canadian Journal of History* 7 (1972), pp.97–8, 103–4, 111.
20. Vivian R. Gruder, '"No Taxation without Representation": The Assembly of Notables of 1787 and Political Ideology in France,' *Legislative History Quarterly* 7 (1982), pp.265, 275.
21. Louis Marie Victor Galard-Magnas, *Compte-rendu des séances de l'administration provinciale d'Auch* (Agen, 1887), p.36; *Procès-verbal des séances de la première assemblée provinciale de la généralité de Lyon*, pp.21, 55–6, 60; *Procès-Verbal des séances de l'Assemblée Provinciale de L'Isle de France* (Sens, 1788), pp.38–9, 41, 320–1, 336–7, 363–5.
22. Rafe Blaufarb, 'Noble Tax Exemptions and the Long-Term Origins of the French Revolution: The Example of Provence, 1530 to 1789,' in Jay Smith (ed.), *The French Nobility in the Eighteenth Century: Reassessments and New Approaches* (University Park, 2006), pp.146–7, 155–7, 159–63; Kwass, *Privilege and the Politics of Taxation*, pp.121, 179, 196, 202, 322.
23. David Parker, 'Absolutism, Feudalism and Property Rights in the France of Louis XIV,' *Past and Present,* 179 (2003), pp.60–96; Thomas Kaiser, 'Property, Sovereignty, the Declaration of the Rights of Man, and the Tradition of French Jurisprudence,' in Dale Van Kley (ed.), *The French Idea of Freedom: The Old Regime and the Declaration of Rights of 1789* (Stanford, 1994), pp.309–10, 312–15.
24. René Crozet, *Histoire du Poitou* (Paris, 1949), pp.80, 97; Georges Bordonove, *Histoire du Poitou* (Paris, 1973), p.275; Pierre Goubert, 'Les fondements démographiques' and 'Société traditionelle et société nouvelle,' in Ernest Labrousse et al. (eds), *Histoire économique et sociale de la France* (Paris, 1970), pp.91, 584. The average income of a rural household was 200 to 300 *livres* a year.
25. Robert Harding, *Anatomy of a Power Elite: The Provincial Governors of Early Modern France* (New Haven, 1978), pp.9, 118, 124, 196–7, 202–3; Swann, *Provincial Power and Absolute Monarchy: The Estates General of Burgundy*, pp.43, 51–2, 66, 110–11.
26. Maurice Garden, *Lyon et les Lyonnais au XVIIIe siècle* (Paris, 1970), pp.491–2; Bayard, 'Les pouvoirs dans la ville', pp.93, 95–6, 98, 102.
27. *Archives Départementales du Rhône (ADR)* 1C46; Julian Swann, *Politics and the Parlement of Paris under Louis XV, 1754–1774* (Cambridge, 1995), pp.196, 255,

261, 268, 270.
28. Parker, 'Absolutism, Feudalism and Property Rights,' pp.85–6, 91–2; Gérard Aubin, *La seigneurie en Bordelais au XVIIIe siècle d'après la pratique notariale: 1715–1789* (Rouen, 1989), pp.180, 381, 388, 394, 400–1, 446–7, 449; Guy Lemarchand, *La fin du féodalisme dans le pays de Caux* (Paris, 1989), pp.21, 294–5, 313–15, 328–9; Peter McPhee, *Revolution and Environment in Southern France: Peasants, Lords and Murder in the Corbières* (Oxford, 1999), pp.26–8, 33–4; Robert Forster, *The House of Saulx-Tavanes; Versailles and Burgundy, 1700–1830* (Baltimore, 1971), pp.92–104; Peter Jones, *Politics and Rural Society: The Southern Massif Central, c. 1750–1880* (Cambridge, 1985), p.163; Florence Gauthier, *La voie paysanne dans la Révolution française: l'exemple de la Picardie* (Paris, 1977), pp.80–1, 83.
29. David Parker, *Class and State in Ancien Régime France: The Road to Modernity?* (London, 1996), pp.176–82; Swann, *Provincial Power and Absolute Monarchy: The Estates General of Burgundy*, pp.12–13, 300, 327; Campbell, *Power and Politics in Old Regime France*, pp.304, 315.
30. William Beik, *Absolutism and Society in Seventeenth-Century France: State Power and Provincial Aristocracy in Languedoc* (Cambridge, 1985); Stephen Miller, *State and Society in Eighteenth-Century France: A Study of Political Power and Social Revolution in Languedoc* (Washington, DC, 2008), pp.57–99.
31. Swann, *Provincial Power and Absolute Monarchy: The Estates General of Burgundy*, pp.57, 65, 110–11, 204, 299, 301–2, 327–8, 409; Mark Potter, *Corps and Clienteles: Public Finance and Political Change in France 1688–1715* (Aldershot, 2003), pp.13–14, 132; James Collins, *Classes, Estates, and Order in Early Modern Brittany* (Cambridge, 1994), pp.175, 283; Armand Rebillon, *Les états de Bretagne de 1661 à 1789* (Paris, 1932), pp.80, 82, 85, 96; Michel Nassiet, *Noblesse et pauvreté: la petite noblesse en Bretagne XVe–XVIIIe siècle* (Mayenne, 1997), p.351.
32. Garden, *Lyon et les Lyonnais au XVIIIe siècle*, pp.190–1, 204, 388–91, 394–7; Roger Chartier, 'L'académie de Lyon au XVIIIe siècle: étude de sociologie culturelle,' in Chartier et al. (eds) *Nouvelle études lyonnaises* (Geneva, 1969), pp.165–6, 173–5.
33. Archives Nationales (AN) P5192 and P5194; Philip Benedict, 'French Cities from the Sixteenth Century to the Revolution: An Overview' and Frederick Irvine, 'From Renaissance City to *Ancien Régime* Capital: Montpellier, c.1500–c.1600,' in Benedict (ed.) *Cities and Social Change in Early Modern France* (London, 1989), pp.29, 112–14; Robert Descimon and Christian Jouhaud, *La France du premier XVIIe siècle: 1594–1661* (Paris, 1996), pp.189–95; William Doyle, *Venality: The Sale of Offices in Eighteenth-Century France* (Oxford, 1996), pp.92, 94, 97, 203–7, 222, 224, 226, 228–30, 232–7; Yves Durand, *Les fermiers généraux au XVIIIe siècle* (Paris, 1971), pp.163–4, 167; Bosher, *French Finances 1770–1795*, pp.174, 304–5.
34. Adrien Bonvallet, 'Le bureau des finances de la généralité de Poitiers,' *Mémoires de la Société des antiquaires de l'Oeust*, VI, 2nd series (1883), pp.191–2, 208–9, 212, 215–21; Dale Van Kley, *The Religious Origins of the French Revolution: From Calvin*

to the *Civil Constitution, 1560–1791* (New Haven, 1996), 145–51; Campbell, *Power and Politics in Old Regime France*, p.278.
35. Jay Smith, *Nobility Reimagined: The Patriotic Nation in Eighteenth-Century France* (Ithaca, 2005), pp.15–16, 98–9, 155, 186, 212–13, 216, 227, 231–2, 263; *Procès-verbaux des séances des corps municipaux de la ville de Lyon…1787–an VIII* (Lyon, 1899–), 1:57–9; Paul Metzger, *Contribution à l'étude de deux réformes judiciares au XVIIIe siècle: le Conseil supérieur et le Grand bailliage de Lyon, 1771–1774, 1788* (Lyon, 1913), pp.297–8; David Andress, *The French Revolution and the People* (London, 2004), pp.71–2; John Markoff, *The Abolition of Feudalism: Peasants, Lords, and Legislators in the French Revolution* (University Park, PA, 1996), pp.126–9.
36. ADR 8 C 236; Arlette Jouanna, *Le devoir de révolte: la noblesse française et la gestation de l'Etat moderne, 1559–1661* (Paris, 1989), pp.12, 62, 114, 116, 267–8, 270; Doyle, *Venality*, pp.269, 276–8; Roland Mousnier, *Social Hierarchies, 1450 to the Present*, trans. Peter Evans (New York,1973).
37. William Beik, *Absolutism and Society in Seventeenth-Century France: State Power and Provincial Aristocracy in Languedoc*, pp.82–3, 176, 185, 197, 219, 304; Sharon Kettering, *Judicial Politics and Urban Revolt in Seventeenth-Century France: The Parlement of Aix, 1629–1659* (Princeton, 1978), pp.41, 46, 57, 59–71, 213, 220, 330–2, 336; Campbell, *Power and Politics in Old Regime France*, pp.308–9.
38. Joël Félix, *Finances et politique au siècle des Lumières: le ministère L'Averdy, 1763–1768* (Paris, 1999), pp.34–5, 298–301, 304, 498–9; Doyle, *Venality*, pp.99–100; Guy Chaussinand-Nogaret, *Les financiers de Languedoc au XVIIIe siècle* (Paris, 1970), pp.11, 237–8, 248–50, 257–8, 261, 263, 265, 312–13.
39. Marion, *Histoire financière de la France depuis 1715*, 1:472–5; Marie-Laure Legay, 'Le credit des provinces au secours de l'état: les emprunts des états provinciaux pour le comte du roi (France, XVIII siècle),' in Françoise Bayard (ed.) *Pourvoir les finances en province sous l'ancien régime* (Paris, 2003), pp.153–4; François Velde and David Weir, 'The Financial Market and Government Debt Policy in France, 1746–1793,' *The Journal of Economic History*, 52 (1992), pp.33–4; Miller, *State and Society in Eighteenth-Century France: A Study of Political Power and Social Revolution in Languedoc*, p.106.
40. Félix, *Finances et politique au siècle des Lumières*, p.499; Miller, *State and Society in Eighteenth-Century France: A Study of Political Power and Social Revolution in Languedoc*, pp.109–33; Hilton Root, *Peasants and King in Burgundy: Agrarian Foundations of French Absolutism* (Berkeley, 1987), pp.2–3, 12, 15, 20–1, 48–50, 61, 64, 192–3, 197; Jean-Laurent Rosenthal, *The Fruits of Revolution: Property Rights, Litigation, and French Agriculture, 1700–1860* (Cambridge, 1992), pp.14, 73, 133.
41. Doyle, *Venality*, pp.107–8, 112, 121; Miller, *State and Society in Eighteenth-Century France: A Study of Political Power and Social Revolution in Languedoc*, pp.133–6.
42. Root, *Peasants and King in Burgundy*, pp.45–7; Rosenthal, *The Fruits of Revolution: Property Rights*, pp.18, 87–8, 94–6, 134–5; Miller, *State and Society in Eighteenth-Century France: A Study of Political Power and Social Revolution in Languedoc*, pp.138–40, 144–8.
43. AN H1134; Eugene Courbis, *Municipalité lyonnaise sous l'ancien régime* (Lyon,

1900), pp.120–2; Jean Pierre Gutton, *Histoire de Lyon et du Lyonnais* (Paris, 1998), pp.75–6; Bossenga, *The Politics of Privilege: Old Regime and Revolution in Lille*, pp.25, 28–30, 37, 40, 46, 76, 80, 88, 90.

44. Parker, *Class and State in Ancien Régime France*, pp.83–7, 100–1; Jean Nicolas, *La rebellion française: mouvements populaires et conscience sociale 1661–1789* (Paris, 2002), pp.56, 120; Galard-Magnas, *Compte-rendu des séances de l'administration provinciale d'Auch*, pp.50–1, 61; Miller, *State and Society in Eighteenth-Century France: A Study of Political Power and Social Revolution in Languedoc*, pp.72–3, 75–8, 97–8, 272.

45. Miller, *State and Society in Eighteenth-Century France: A Study of Political Power and Social Revolution in Languedoc*, pp.60–6; Lenard Berlanstein, *The Barristers of Toulouse in the Eighteenth Century (1740–1793)* (Baltimore, 1975), pp.40, 53, 112, 149, 161–2, 168–9; Sarah Maza, *Private Lives and Public Affairs: The Causes Célèbres of Prerevolutionary France* (Berkeley, 1993), pp.13, 256, 319; Bell, *Lawyers and Citizens*, pp.12, 89, 163, 169.

46. Swann, *Provincial Power and Absolute Monarchy: The Estates General of Burgundy*, pp.24–5, 373, 377, 388, 410; Miller, *State and Society in Eighteenth-Century France: A Study of Political Power and Social Revolution in Languedoc*, pp.144–53.

47. Ch-L Chassin, *La préparation de la guerre de Vendée, 1789–1793* (Paris, 1892), pp.28–30; H. Beauchet-Filleau and P. Beauchet-Filleau, *Tiers-Etat du Poitou en 1789: procès-verbaux, cahier des doléances* (Paris, 1989), pp.94, 101–2, 116–19, 126–7; Markoff, *The Abolition of Feudalism*, pp.30–1, 35–6.

48. Marcel Bruneau, *Les débuts de la Révolution dans les départements du Cher et de l'Indre: 1789–1791* (Geneva, 1977), pp.26–8, 34; Henri Beauchet-Filleau, *Noblesse du Poitou en 1789: procès-verbaux, cahier des doléances* (France, 1990), p.168. See also pages 164–5, 167, 169–70, 172. Markoff, *The Abolition of Feudalism*, pp.79, 81, 87.

Revolution or *Jacquerie*?
Rethinking Peasant Insurrection in 1789

Peter McPhee

For several decades following Georges Lefebvre's pioneering studies of the nature and outcomes of the French Revolution some seventy years ago, historians agreed that, while peasant involvement had its own impulses and rhythms, it constituted a genuine revolutionary upheaval at the heart of the Revolution itself.[1] While some subsequently furthered Alfred Cobban's famous critique of Lefebvre and his Jacobin-Marxist successors in denying that there was a deep-seated and revolutionary crisis in rural France, most 'revisionist' historians have since been far more interested in pursuing élite political history or in identifying the new urban behaviours and discursive assumptions which sapped the foundations of the social and political system we call the *Ancien Régime*.[2] Other historians have seen the Revolution as an inchoate popular upheaval ultimately tamed by a new and more resolute state system. According to David Andress, for example, there were no identifiable popular ideologies well into 1789: the dramatic events in rural France were simply an expression of basic material grievances. Even by July of that year, he writes, 'the peasants and workers of France were not motivated by any revolutionary ideology'.[3] Donald Sutherland has gone so far as to argue that the Revolution was 'largely an urban phenomenon'.[4] In contrast, Serge Bianchi, Jean Boutier, Jean-Pierre Jessenne, Peter Jones, John Markoff, Gilbert Shapiro and others have continued to find in detailed analysis of rural social relations a central element of the narrative of revolution.[5] For them, peasant participation in 1789 and beyond was based on revolutionary assumptions about power and justice within specific local contexts.

Are the extraordinary events in the French countryside in 1789 best understood as only the spectacular culmination of a long history of atavistic peasant rebellions (*jacqueries*) against the visible causes of misery (such as tax-collectors, seigneurial officials, and engrossers of private property) or instead as a revolutionary assault on a whole social and political system?

One way of answering this question is to examine the 'lists of grievances' (*cahiers de doléances*) required of rural parishes in Louis XVI's calling of the Estates-General and drawn up by rural parishes in the late winter and early spring of 1789. Even though there are significant limitations to their utility as statements of the attitudes of rural inhabitants, the many thousands of these *cahiers* which are still extant are an unparalleled source for the historian of peasant attitudes on the eve of the Revolution. After all, these were not *post facto* statements of revolutionary zeal but responses to the king's request for his people's views.

The formulation of *cahiers* in more than 40,000 parishes across the kingdom followed six months of acute anxiety in the face of a crisis in the food supply, due to the impact of drought, then summer storms, on the 1788 harvest. The following winter was unusually severe across the whole country, and the high price of firewood further undermined the capacity of rural wage earners to procure sufficient food. In such a situation rural communities, particularly in the northern half of the kingdom, had recourse to direct action to ensure their survival. Such collective action was neither unprecedented nor inherently revolutionary. The history of rural France had been studded with protest; indeed, Guy Lemarchand has calculated that in the years 1720–88 there were no fewer than 4,400 collective protests significant enough to be documented, some three-quarters of them after 1765.[6] These protests were of three main types: food riots, and riots against taxation and seigneurialism. All of them were designed to repel the personification of external threats to the rural community at moments of vulnerability: such as a merchant or large farmer taking a wagon of grain to market, a seigneur's agent making exactions that were novel or had fallen into disuse, or a tax official without sufficient protection.

These were all protests within a system which people assumed would never end. In the spring of 1789, however, people in small towns and villages began behaving and voicing attitudes in ways which challenged the structures of their world in unprecedented ways, through more open confrontation with seigneurs and other local élites. For, as winter dragged into spring, the sharp edge of hunger and anxiety coincided with the elation and expectation occasioned by Louis XVI's calling of the *Estates-General*. Uncertain about the future, peasants at least knew that the sudden vulnerability of seigneurs had opened up a moment in which boundaries could be further tested. The open political debates of early 1789 encouraged peasants to abandon their traditional tactics of dissembling and manoeuvring against authority and instead to be direct about what James Scott has called their usually 'hidden transcript'.[7] For had not the King declared that he wished to hear his people's grievances? Peasants now had the perfect pretext and excuse for bolder actions.

Since December 1788, peasants had refused to pay taxes or dues or had seized food supplies in parts of the Cambrésis and Hainaut regions in the northeast, the Franche-Comté, and the Paris basin, partly perhaps in expectation of royal recognition of their plight. Such actions were sporadic and local, but everywhere the anxiety over food supplies coincided with unprecedented opportunities to participate in political life as men in villages and country towns all over France met to formulate proposals for the regeneration of public life in the *cahiers* and to elect deputies to the Estates-General. The drawing up of the *cahiers* in the context of political uncertainty, fiscal emergency and subsistence crisis was for the rural population the first episode in a decade of revolution. They would come to know that only in retrospect, of course, just as it is only from hindsight that the coincidence of economic crisis and political opportunity appears to historians as the decisive moment in the mass politicisation of social friction in the countryside.

The calling of the Estates-General and the convocation of assemblies to frame the *cahiers* reverberated at every level of society. The electoral provisions for the Estates-General announced on 24 January were far broader than the property qualifications imposed on local government elections by the edict of the Controller-General Calonne in June 1787: all adult male tax-payers in the countryside were eligible to attend special parish meetings which were to agree on the content of the *cahier* and to appoint delegates, usually two to four depending on the size of the parish, to represent it at district (*bailliage* or *sénéchaussée*) level. The responsibilities of municipal councils were restricted to local matters; now the health of the kingdom was a matter for popular debate. Millions of rural households which had hitherto experienced the structures of power and privilege as constraints to be obeyed, sidestepped or occasionally contested were now authorised, even required, to reflect on their efficacy and legitimacy and to identify and suggest remediation for their grievances.[8]

The tens of thousands of parish *cahiers* ranged in length from many pages of detailed criticisms and suggestions in larger villages and country towns to the three sentences written in a mixture of French and Catalan from the tiny village of Serrabone in the stony foothills of the Pyrenees. While there is no better source for understanding popular attitudes in early 1789, there are three important limits to their utility and transparency as direct statements of the views of the commoners of the countryside. A first limitation is that many of the *cahiers* of rural parishes were influenced by a generic or model document, usually emanating from a nearby town.[9] For example, in the *bailliage* of Amont in eastern France, scores of parishes reproduced a statement demanding that 'all forges, furnaces and factories established in the province of Franche-Comté within the past thirty years be destroyed as well as older ones whose proprietors do not personally possess a forest large enough to power them for six months per year.'[10] Many of the *cahiers* of parishes between Narbonne and Carcassonne in Languedoc were similarly influenced by a *cahier* which seems to have been produced in Narbonne, but the parish assemblies almost always added some articles of their own. At Moux, for example, the *cahier* reproduced 26 articles from the model, but these were interspersed with 8 less polished but more forceful clauses.[11] Further around the Mediterranean, half of the 346 *cahiers* in the *sénéchausée* of Nîmes used clauses from circulated *cahiers*, but none contented themselves with simply making a copy.[12] Indeed, rather than reflecting unthinking peasant acquiescence in reproducing a model *cahier*, the common reiteration of specific articles was due to the resonance of particular issues.

A second limit to the usefulness of the *cahiers* is that they were often compiled under direct/indirect forms of intimidation from priests, seigneurs or their agents. Even where the influence of *curés* and seigneurial agents was benign, it may have hindered the *cahiers* from being transparent representations of peasant attitudes, for example, when the *curé* or local professional such as a lawyer acted as an intermediary in formalising vigorous discussion into ordered text.[13] The economically dependent in small rural communities were acutely aware of the potential costs of outspoken criticism of noble privilege and prerogative. In the impoverished village of Erceville, north of Orléans, for example, the parish assembly was presided over by the local judge employed by the seigneur, a prominent member of the parlement (high court) of Paris whose holdings covered most of the parish (seigneurial judges presided over 53 per cent of village assemblies in the Orléanais). Not surprisingly, his tenants decided to stay away from the meeting. Nevertheless, the peasants, labourers and artisans who did attend to draw up Erceville's *cahier* were remarkably bold, requiring the magistrate to write articles stipulating that, 'without any distinction of title or rank, the said seigneur be taxed like them', that 'the tithe and the *champart* (harvest due) be abolished, or at least converted into an annual payment in money', and—clearly aware of the looming political issue of whether the three orders would deliberate separately or jointly at Versailles—that all taxes should require 'the consent of the whole Nation assembled in Estates-General'.[14]

A final constraint on the transparency of the *cahiers* is that, although in theory all male taxpayers over 25 years of age were eligible to participate in the process of drawing them up, their compilation was likely to be—whether or not by general consent—in the hands of the better-off minority of villagers. For example, not only was the *cahier* of La Vallée-Foulon near Reims composed in the intimidating presence of the abbey of Vauclair's legal officer and seigneurial agent, it was drawn up by the better-off inhabitants (it was signed by only 10 men from the 32 households in the village). It is perhaps not surprising that it expressed boundless gratitude to the abbey for the land and houses it made available for rent—'they declare that they have no complaint to make'—and put 'their full confidence in the paternal goodness of His Majesty'.[15] Elsewhere we know that others who could not sign were in fact present. The twelve surviving Third Estate *cahiers* from the Corbières region of Languedoc concluded with the formula that 'the literate members have signed', but the records of the meetings show that many more men in fact were present than indicated by the numbers of those who could sign, as many as 85 per cent of male heads of household at Cruscades.[16] In any case, at least until 1790 consensus within rural communities about major grievances tended to disguise frictions within the peasantry (typically between larger farmers and the almost landless) and between peasants and others (such as artisans and professional men) in larger village communities.

Historians have often questioned the usefulness of the *cahiers* because of these limitations, but they remain of unparalleled value in indicating the attitudes and tensions in rural France on the eve of the Revolution. Every parish expressed grievances which tell us something of the specifics of a local community, but what is most remarkable is the similarity of major grievances across the country. The *cahiers* reveal that the fundamental issue everywhere was that of control of resources and the claims of the crown and the privileged over those resources. The interaction between rural people and their local environment was mediated through a complex of social relationships which had evolved across eight centuries. All land worked by peasants—whether or not they owned it—was subject to the claims of others: the king, the Catholic Church, seigneurs, and other households in the community. Few peasants owned enough land for their household's survival, and even when they did their labours had also to meet royal taxes, the church tithe, and a maze of seigneurial and other exactions. An example of how severe these could be comes from the village of Pomas, a few kilometres south of the cloth-manufacturing town of Carcassonne. Its seigneuresse was Catherine de Poulpry, the granddaughter of a very wealthy textile magnate who had bought nobility in 1720, and who then amassed 23 seigneuries and 45 large properties before his death in 1725. From Pomas in the 1780s the marquise de Poulpry collected 2,113 *livres* worth of seigneurial dues at a time when a labourer's wage was about one *livre* per day; the dues included 99 *setiers* (a *setier* was about 85 litres) of wheat, rye, millet, barley and oats, 126 chickens, 5 capons, 2 pairs of gloves and a pound of beeswax. These exactions were in fact lighter for Pomas than the church's tithe (3,970 *livres*), which was divided between the parish priest, the bishop of Carcassonne, the local seminary and the cathedral chapter (which also took 2½ *setiers* of barley and five capons). The church and seigneur together took perhaps one-fifth of the produce of the community as a direct exaction: these exactions amounted to perhaps 60 *livres* for each of the one hundred or so families of Pomas. In addition, state taxes took perhaps another 15 per cent and the private land Poulpry had in Pomas brought her another 8,000 *livres* a year in rent and produce, perhaps one-quarter of the village's wealth. By the 1780s Catherine de Poulpry had long tired of life in Carcassonne and had become lady-in-waiting to Marie-Antoinette's sister-in-law, with a fine house in the Faubourg Saint-Germain in Paris. But she ensured her estates were run with a tight hand.[17]

In all, the exactions of the royal state, the Church and seigneurs amounted to as little as about 14 per cent of what a peasant household might produce in Brittany (8 per cent as tithe, 4 per cent as taxes and 2 per cent as seigneurial dues) to perhaps 40 per cent elsewhere.[18] The main harvest due—variously known as the *champart, tasque, censive* or *tierce*—varied from just one-twentieth in the Dauphiné to as much as one-third in the Limousin: an average figure for the whole country would be one-sixth, but rates varied even on lands within the same parish. Seigneurial dues were everywhere a central concern in the *cahiers*, even in Brittany, and could be complex as well as onerous.

John Markoff and Gilbert Shapiro have analysed 1,112 of the 40,000 *cahiers*, among them 748 from village communities.[19] Their exhaustive quantitative analysis demonstrated that the most common parish complaints concerned taxation exemptions, the structure and powers of the Estates-General, and indirect taxes. The economic power and seigneurial 'rights' fiercely guarded by the nobility and religious orders were a constant dimension of rural life: querulous references to them pervade the *cahiers*. Harvest dues were the most significant issues, but there were frequent references to other 'rights', such as the monopoly (*banalité*) over the village oven, grape and olive press, and mill; the irregular payments in some areas when peasants acquired land or married; and the obligatory unpaid labour by the community on the lord's lands.

Although more than three-quarters of the village *cahiers* criticised seigneurialism, Markoff and Shapiro have demonstrated that a more common target of peasant anger in 1789 was state taxation. The issues were closely linked, however, for what rankled most with commoners was the privileged fiscal treatment of the noble élite, whether seigneurs or as bishops and abbots within the Church. Typical in this regard was the *cahier* of the parish of Sagy in the Vexin region to the north of Paris, situated between the Seine and Oise rivers. Its chief targets were the burden of state taxes on commoners, and noble hunting and other privileges: they wanted 'to pay taxes in proportion to their capacity, with the clergy and nobility, and to enjoy in freedom the cultivation of their land without being troubled by any form of servitude'.[20] This connection made between noble privilege and state taxes is a critical point for, even if historians have seen in the impulses of the royal state to centralise and make uniform the justice system, for example, a means by which royal 'protection' was increasingly within the reach of the peasantry,[21] rural communities rarely made a distinction between royal office holders, seigneurs and upper clergy as elements of an oppressive hierarchy of power.

Peasant *cahiers* did, however, make a distinction between royal and seigneurial courts. While in northern Burgundy and upper Brittany, for example, the role of seigneurs in administering justice seems to have been regarded as a respected element of village life which considered far more than the lord's interests, elsewhere their courts were seen to be expensive, inefficient and primarily concerned to maintain the property and privileges of the nobility and church.[22] This was a particular concern in the province of Berry, where the parish of Levet (like many others) requested that 'seigneurial justice be abolished and those called to justice instead plead before the closest royal judge'. Similarly, in his study of the western provinces of Aunis and Saintonge, Anthony Crubaugh has shown that the system of seigneurial justice was a constant presence in the countryside and resented as costly, slow and preoccupied with the protection of noble privilege and status. The royal *sénéchaussée* of St Jean d'Angély, for example, had 171 seigneurial courts for its 146 parishes. Twenty-four cases that Crubaugh studied in the community of Tonnay-Boutonne required on average 32 months to resolve, and peasant plaintiffs were further dissuaded by the expense of protracted proceedings. A peasant maxim in the region was that 'a bad arrangement is better than a good trial'; the *cahier* from Landraye agreed: 'it's the fable of the wolf and the lamb'. From the other side of the country, in Lorraine, the *cahier* of Dolving complained bitterly that 'under such justice the people can never be anything but a hopeless victim of the most disastrous rapacity and pillage', and called the courts a 'sad residue of the feudal regime'.[23]

While some historians have concluded that the 'feudal reaction'—whereby seigneurs revisited registers of dues payable (*terriers*) to increase peasant obligations—was a post-revolutionary myth, the allegation in some *cahiers* that seigneurs were becoming more rapacious is supported by local case-studies. Aunis and Saintonge were regions where harvest dues were commonly levied at one-sixth or one-seventh of produce and commonly constituted about one-half of the revenues of seigneurs (in one case 87 per cent). Crubaugh found that at least 39 seigneuries in these regions revised their registers in the period 1750–89.[24] Hostility to seigneurial exactions tended to go together with criticism of the tithes, fees and practices of the Church; that is, they were seen as interdependent within the seigneurial regime. Across the country the level of the tithe ranged from as little as 3 per cent in Provence and Dauphiné in the southeast, in the Auvergne and around Vannes in Brittany to about one-sixth in parts of the Franche-Comté. On average, the tithe took one-twelfth of local produce. In some regions, such as the countryside around Auch in Gascony or in the mountainous lands around Amont in Franche-Comté the tithe was particularly heavy and criticism of it was omnipresent in the *cahiers*.[25] Most commonly, however, it was the collection of the tithe by distant religious orders and cathedral chapters, rather than the levy *per se*, which was the target of peasant resentment.

The *cahiers* reveal how central were disputes pertaining to control over resources, for across the country parish assemblies focused on grievances about common lands, pasturing rights, access to and ownership of forests, and who was responsible for excessive land clearances, erosion and flooding.[26] Everywhere, the way rural communities described their world was a function of their understanding of the proper use of physical resources, and the targets of their criticism were those seen to be exercising excessive private control, whether manufacturers or seigneurs.[27] In the *bailliage* of Vic, near Metz, the royal saltworks at Dieuze, Moyenvic and Château-Salins were especially singled out for criticism because they consumed vast quantities of wood to produce a salt which was in any case more expensive than sea-salt.[28] In Lorraine, the *cahiers* were virtually unanimous in their condemnation both of the impact of industries and of the complicity of noble forest owners and royal administrators in supplying wood to private industry at the expense of rural communities. It was this, argued the commoners of Guébestroff, which forced the poor to damage forests further by illegal cutting of trees.[29] The parish of Brouville claimed that 'these wood-fired factories have caused a great devastation in the forests which mostly belong to the bishop of Metz, and whose guards scarcely observe the laws concerning forests.'[30]

It was not only forge owners who were the targets of peasant anger: antipathy to allegedly rapacious industrialists was often linked to anti-seigneuralism, as local seigneurs were charged with having abdicated their community responsibilities in order to furnish fuel to industry. Around Quimper and Tréguier in Brittany, seigneurs and large landowners were singled out as primarily responsible for a shortage of wood, and oppressive of those in need.[31] The *cahier* of Plozévet expressed a very common point of view:

> The poor vassal who has the misfortune to cut a foot off a tree of little value, but of which he has great need for a house or a cart or a plough, is plagued and crushed by his seigneur for the value of a whole tree. If everybody had the right to plant and to cut for oneself, without being able to sell, there would not be so much loss of wood.[32]

Such resentments were aggravated by the nobility's perceived taste for luxury consumption. The Third Estate of Dosches (*bailliage* of Troyes) complained that 'the poor person is rightly alarmed; he sees with indignation the wastefulness of the rich who, by the multitude of their fires, consume a terrifying volume of wood'.[33] From Juvaincourt, it was argued that the seigneur's taste for luxury was a poor example to the community: apart from the kitchen, there were 'five or six fires that *monsieur* needs, as many for *madame*, the children's fires (one for each of course), those for the servants of both sexes'.[34]

Like local seigneurs, the agents of the royal state were frequently charged with complicity in the degradation of collective resources.[35] Many communities near Châlons-sur-Marne were convinced that royal officials based in the region ostensibly to ensure sustainable tree-felling were in fact protecting 'the greed of the beneficiaries' of the new glass- and brick-works.[36] The *cahier* of Sainte-Anne in the *bailliage* of Metz went as far as to call for the domains belonging to the Church and the king to be sold 'or at least rented in small lots; an individual would know well how to conserve a forest near his home…'.[37] 'If the province governed itself', claimed the *cahier* of Forcelles-sous-Gugney, 'it would be better able to act effectively' to conserve the forests.[38]

Despite the intimidation which seigneurs and their agents were able to exert, the boldness of vulnerable rural people was at times startling. A rare recording of events in one parish was compiled by Pierre-Louis-Nicolas Delahaye (born in 1745), the schoolteacher and parish clerk of the village of Silly-en-Multien, near Senlis. From 1771 Delahaye kept a record of 'remarkable and curious events'; it was he who wrote down the parish *cahier* in February 1789. The seigneur of Silly was the Prince de Conti, and the village was subject to the requirements of the prince's hunting estate. The *cahier* was a long series of complaints against the vulnerability of the crops to the prince's game and of villagers to his guards' whims: the villagers still recalled that in 1768 a woman who took a pheasant's egg had been thrown into prison. In the midst of a series of very specific complaints in the *cahier* was inserted a sweeping statement from which two nervous village notables promptly disassociated themselves: 'What advantage for the public good if the hunting codes and feudal dues were abolished, that there were no *banalités*, in a word that the French regained their liberty'.[39] Peasants elsewhere took the opportunity to highlight to the king what seemed to be humiliating 'rights', for example, that requiring the inhabitants of Moimay, near Vesoul in the east, to beat the seigneur's ponds at night when the croaking of frogs was too loud.[40] From the southernmost corner of the kingdom, the few lines submitted from the impoverished hamlet of Périllos in the stony *garrigues* of the Corbières were bluntly hostile to the seigneurial system: 'This community is very poor because we don't have the same rights and privileges as do others; the Seigneur treats us like slaves'.[41]

Men long used to the exercise of power in the countryside were startled by the boldness of rural communities and the language with which the charged political context of early 1789 had invested their grievances. From the village of Pont-sur-Seine in Champagne a seigneur's agent wrote to his master:

> In vain I've done everything I can to exclude from the *cahier* the articles on the abolition of *banalités*, of the right to hunt, and other seigneurial dues…The intention and the tenacity of the people are immovable on this question and it is impossible to dissuade them, because they have been given the right to express their grievances.[42]

New assumptions of rights and citizenship were not only expressed in provinces close to Paris. Most rural people spoke a language other than French in daily life, such as Occitan, Breton, Basque or Flamand, and many lived in provinces such as Lorraine or Roussillon only recently incorporated into the kingdom. Despite a lively sense of regional difference, their rural *cahiers* expressed an assumption of French citizenship within a regenerated nation.[43] Such evidence suggests that 1789 was not the sudden rupture in peasant outlook and values so often assumed by historians, but rather a long time in the moulding and the result of complex social interactions.

In the Occitan-speaking Corbières region of Lower Languedoc, for example, there were frequent hopes expressed for a reformed and permanent provincial Estates, following the model of the Dauphiné, but none of the *cahiers* asserted that Languedoc should enjoy a measure of special autonomy. Instead, words like 'patrie', 'nation' and 'citoyen' were studded throughout the *cahiers*, which were imbued with assumptions of a secular citizenship as the basis of a regenerated public realm. The peasants of the region had developed an understanding of society as composed of people of equal dignity, articulated in the repeated call from practising Catholics that the king accord his 'non-Catholic subjects the civic status and prerogatives of French citizens', which was based on 'civil and individual liberty for all citizens'.[44] It was here that a year later the baron de Bouisse, seigneur of the tiny village of Fraïsse, despaired that new French words had entered the peasants' Occitan:

> I have cherished and I still cherish the people of Fraïsse as I have cherished my own children; they were so sweet and so honest in their way, but what a sudden change has taken place among them. All I hear now is *corvée, lanternes, démocrates, aristocrates*, words which for me are barbaric and which I can't use...the former vassals believe themselves to be more powerful than Kings.[45]

Immediately to the south in the Roussillon, Catalans had been incorporated in the French state for only 130 years, but there too the existence of the French polity was now taken for granted. Vingrau, one of the communities on the very frontier with Languedoc, insisted both that the two provinces should be divided by 'visible and permanent' markers but at the same time that all taxes and charges should be uniform throughout the kingdom, despite the fact that the commoners of the Roussillon were taxed more lightly than their Occitan neighbours.[46]

In some areas the formulation of the *cahiers* was only part of a spectrum of community action which extended into open rebellion. Food rioting in Cambrai spread to the surrounding countryside early in May 1789, where a dozen communities around Oisy slaughtered a lord's game. In Provence, peasants from around Draguignan drove their cattle onto the estate of the Count de Gallifet, apparently in a deliberate action to ruin his crops.[47] In the Périgord, there was a full-scale attack on the château of Saint-Léon-d'Issigeac. In this region a series of violent incidents in 1789 involved a cross-section of rural communities: substantial landowners, sharecroppers, winegrowers, rural labourers and artisans, with occasionally a country doctor (*chirurgien-barbier*) or lawyer. Their enemies were primarily seigneurs and their agents, but also well-to-do bourgeois proprietors. As one peasant from Alassac put it: 'We don't need bourgeois or gentlemen any more'.[48]

We should hesitate before assuming that such frank hostility only developed or was expressed in 1789, for historians have located abundant evidence of a greater willingness to contest authority in the countryside in the decades before the Revolution. Nicole and Yves Castan, Olwen Hufton and Georges Fournier have found evidence of young men on the lowlands of Languedoc, for example, more commonly contesting the authority of seigneur, *curé* and local officials, and exhibiting a fractiousness sometimes denounced as a 'republican spirit' by the authorities. Southeast of Carcassonne, a day-labourer from Albas had commented audibly to others as the seigneur passed in 1784: 'If you would do as I do we'd soon put to rights this young__ of a seigneur'. Later he had continued to the local blacksmith, 'If you would all do as I do, not only would you not raise your hats when you pass in front of them, but you wouldn't even recognise them as seigneurs, because as for me I've never and will never in my life raise my hat, they're a huge load of scum, thieves, young…' At nearby Termes a man took his brother-in-law to court years before the Revolution for having said 'that he carried on like a seigneur, with his arrogant tone'.[49]

There had always been moments when young men like this had vented their anger at those in authority. In the spring of 1789, however, the process for the compilation of the *cahiers* gave every member of rural communities explicit permission to comment directly on the world in which they lived and how it might be improved. Evident in their formulation—and all the more telling given the presence of seigneurial judges or stewards at many parish assemblies—was the self-assurance of the village élites who dominated the drawing up of the *cahiers*. These élites, of better-off farmers and, in large villages, artisans, professional men and officials, assumed that their social influence was matched by their right to speak directly on local matters and not through a seigneurial or ecclesiastical intermediary.[50]

At least on the surface, the *cahiers* of all three orders show a remarkable level of agreement: they assumed or requested that the meeting of the Estates-General in May 1789 would be but the first of a regular cycle; and they asserted the need for sweeping reform to taxation, the judiciary, the Church, and the royal administration. On fundamental matters of social order and political power, however, unbridgeable divisions were to undermine the possibilities of consensual reform. Rural communities and their seigneurs were in sharp disagreement about seigneurial dues and a maze of other exactions and privileges, and bourgeois across the country challenged the nobility by advocating 'careers open to talent', equality of taxation, and the ending of privilege. Many parish priests agreed with the commons about taxation reform in particular, and were sympathetic towards peasant grievances, while insisting on the prerogatives of their own order.

The rural inhabitants of France could not have envisaged the consequences of such divisions: Louis XVI had asked his people for their advice and support in a consultative process, not whether they would prefer the end of a complete social and political system. Nevertheless, the invitation to involvement in political life in the spring of 1789 had reverberated across the country: participation in the process of setting out the views in these *cahiers* was an extraordinary experience. To be sure, of themselves the *cahiers* were not explicitly revolutionary: no-one in France in the early spring of 1789 knew that they were about to live through what became in hindsight 'the Revolution of 1789'. Again and again, however, the *cahiers* of the Third Estate had made demands for a regular meeting of a representative body such as the Estates-General, equality of taxation and opportunity, and the end of seigneurialism. Consciously or not, together these demands presupposed the end of a particular social and political order.

After drawing up their *cahiers*, parish assemblies were required to elect two delegates for the first 100 households and one more for each extra 100; the delegates in turn were to elect deputies for each of the 234 constituencies as part of the process of consolidating parish *cahiers* into one for their district. Participation at the parish level was generally high everywhere, but varied sharply, ranging in Upper Normandy from 10 to 88 per cent between parishes, around Béziers from 5 to 83 per cent, near Vitré in Brittany from 6 to 96 per cent, and in Artois from 14 to 97 per cent. In what was to become a common feature of the revolutionary period, such variations were a reflection either of levels of enthusiasm or of the extent to which voters shared a common view about who should or would be elected, that is, whether it was worth voting at all. The parishes tended to elect as delegates those whom they felt would both make a good impression and understand what was going on, such as the larger landowners, artisans, and occasionally professional men and teachers, those who had played a leading role in the actual writing of the *cahiers*.[51]

These district assemblies in local town centres were often confused and stormy occasions, for many urban bourgeois dismissed parish complaints about seigneurial monopolies and other specific grievances as private matters between them and the seigneur. Despite the municipal office experience of many delegates, at the *bailliage* level there was lack of clarity about what was being decided and what those decisions represented: at times peasant delegates assumed that they were deliberative gatherings of the sovereign people. Desmé de Daubuisson, lieutenant-général of the *bailliage* of Saumur on the Loire River, complained that:

> What is really tiresome is that these assemblies that have been summoned have generally believed themselves to be invested with some sovereign authority and that when they came to an end the peasants went home with the idea that henceforward they were free from tithes, hunting prohibitions and the payment of seigneurial dues.[52]

The voting procedures and eligibility requirements for Third Estate deputies, as well as deeply engrained assumptions about education, wealth and capacity, ensured that virtually all of the 646 Third Estate deputies were lawyers, officials and property-owners, men of substance and repute in their town or region. Once the Estates-General opened in Versailles on 4 May, these deputies rapidly developed a common outlook, insistent on their dignity and responsibility to 'the Nation': they refused to meet in a separate Third Estate chamber, and on 17 June proclaimed themselves the National Assembly. This Assembly was only saved from probable dissolution by the direct intervention of Parisian working people, angry at an escalation in the price of bread, and certain that 'their' Assembly was under military threat. Their seizure of the Bastille on 14 July not only saved the National Assembly: it also sent shock-waves across a countryside seething with friction, anxiety, and expectation.

No-one in Versailles or Paris could have imagined the rural response to the news of the taking of the Bastille. Parishes had placed their hopes in the meeting of the Estates-General; now news of the seizure of the fortress tempered such hopes with fears that the nobility would take revenge on the Third Estate and that there would be a breakdown in law and order. During the second half of July villages formed up popular militias. The bands of destitute people roaming country roads were the focus of suspicion as anxious peasants waited for crops to ripen: were the wandering poor possibly in the pay of vengeful nobles conspiring to destroy peasants' crops? Panics fanned out almost simultaneously from sparks in different parts of the country as accounts of suspicious behaviour became magnified into terrifying accounts of armed brigands, these rumours travelling like bushfires from village to village, and affecting every region except Brittany and the east. When the expected noble revenge failed to eventuate, many village militias instead turned their weapons on the seigneurial system itself, invading châteaux in the search for foodstuffs and sometimes compelled seigneurs or their agents to hand over feudal registers to be burned in public.

This unprecedented revolt came to be known as the 'Great Fear'. After the drawing up of the *cahiers de doléances*, this was the second great act of revolution in which masses of rural people were involved. While many local incidents took the traditional form of compelling vulnerable members of the privileged orders or their agents to surrender food, there were at times two new elements: the seizure and destruction of feudal registers, and the public humiliation of seigneurs or their stewards. Unlike the meetings which had produced the *cahiers*, this time those involved in this frontal assault on the seigneurial system were well aware of what they were doing and of the severe consequences of failure. For example, on 24 July the inhabitants of Pont-de-Veyle, just south of Mâcon, besieged the local château and seized the seigneurial registers and other papers, which they deposited at the town hall, symbolic of 'the people's' power. The scene was repeated next day, at nearby Vonnas. Up to eight hundred peasants from twelve villages attacked the abbey at Saint-Sulpice, forcing the monks to burn the registers, and plundering the abbey's cellar. The following day they erected a gibbet in the middle of the cloister, ostensibly to hang the monks, who were allowed finally to flee in terror into the surrounding forest before the insurgents set fire to the buildings.[53]

Pierre Delahaye, the schoolteacher at Silly-en-Multien, near Senlis, described vividly in his journal the snow, rain and hunger of the winter of 1788–9. In late June he recorded that 'we are in frightful distress, all we hear is talk of revolts and massacres everywhere. There is no more wheat to be found.' On 27 July, the Great Fear reached Silly. In Delahaye's words, the inhabitants believed the rumour that harvesters guarded by soldiers were cutting the crops prematurely:

> the alarm was sounded and the priest ran through the village to gather all the men and boys, all armed, a few with rifles, the others with forks, spits, axes, pitchforks, with whatever they could, then left with the priest at their head, wearing his cockade.[54]

In other places, specific targets of local hatred were attacked. In Alsace, Jews were singled out: in Durmenach, Hagenthal and Hegenheim Jewish houses were pillaged.[55] In Flanders and the Cambrésis, where there were 185 monasteries and convents, seven of them were attacked in the last week of July, and two completely pillaged. Hundreds of peasants from Taisnières descended on the Benedictine abbey of Maroilles, which had won expensive court cases against the village in 1757 and 1775 and where early in 1789 the abbot had erected a pillory surmounted by a gibbet on the village square as a warning.[56]

Sometimes rioters used the traditional tactic of self-protection by arguing that they believed they were acting against hoarders on the orders of the king.[57] At other times, they adopted the language of the Third Estate revolt to their own ends. From Montmartin, to the north east of Paris, the steward of the estate of the Duke of Montmorency wrote to his master on 2 August that 'approximately three hundred brigands from all the lands associated with the vassals of Mme the Marquise de Longaunay have stolen the titles of rents and allowances of the seigneurie, and demolished her dovecotes: they then gave her a receipt for the theft signed *The Nation*.'[58]

These images—a priest wearing a revolutionary cockade at the head of a crowd of peasants determined to protect the community against 'brigands' in the pay of aristocrats, the pillaging of Jewish homes and peasants deliberately describing themselves as 'the Nation'—serve to highlight the argument of this article, that the question posed in its title is a false dichotomy. As Clay Ramsay has argued, the Great Fear was driven by 'conservative' impulses to protect local communities against outsiders, but its outcomes were radical, particularly in the creation of popular militias which were far more than appendages of established authority and which in many places violently attacked the seigneurial system.[59]

Rural communities drew on an extensive repertoire of well-tried forms of protest against well-known enemies in 1789, but the ambitions of collective behaviour—legal as well as illegal—had shifted dramatically. It is not that rural inhabitants had somehow developed an ideology where previously their impulses had been atavistic. Just as the specific nature of each community was the result of its own history, so its inhabitants perceived their world through the prism of their own experiences and the orally transmitted memories of others. The *cahiers* are replete with references to the past, ranging from evocations of an imaginary golden age to specific dates when arrangements with seigneurs had been codified or, occasionally, to the lack of care earlier generations had paid to the environment.[60] When they reacted to threats to their well being and opportunities for change in 1788–9 peasants did not do so in a merely mechanical or ideologically empty way: the notion of *jacquerie* itself had been invented by élites who did not comprehend the motivations of peasant riots which terrified them. What was revolutionary about the rural insurrection of 1789 compared with the protests that had always been part of rural life was the confrontation and 'implicit negotiation', in John Markoff's words, between distant political élites and rural communities which facilitated a dramatic rethinking about power, so evident in the *cahiers*, and the waves of rebellion called the Great Fear.[61] Rather than William Doyle's assertion that the rural *cahiers* failed to condemn feudalism outright and that 'such an idea was beyond the intellectual grasp of illiterate or semi-literate peasants', the evidence supports John Markoff's conclusion that they demonstrate 'a thoughtful and nuanced capacity to differentiate among their burdens and that they had their own sort of radicalism'.[62]

The Great Fear was a revolutionary confrontation, and the noble, clerical and bourgeois deputies of the National Assembly were well aware of its import. In an atmosphere of panic, self-sacrifice and exhilaration, a series of nobles mounted the rostrum on 4 August to respond to the crisis in the countryside. The legislators' original intention—to respond to reports of peasant insurrection by abolishing seigneurial dues in return for monetary compensation—was overwhelmed by the panic-stricken surrender of a maze of other privileges. In the succeeding week, however, they made a distinction between instances of 'personal servitude' (serfdom, dovecotes, seigneurial and royal hunting privileges and unpaid labour), which were abolished outright, and 'property rights' (seigneurial dues payable on harvests) for which peasants would have to pay compensation before ceasing payment.[63]

Later in August the Assembly approved the Declaration of the Rights of Man and of the Citizen, together with the August Decrees on Feudalism marking the end of the absolutist, seigneurial and corporate structure of eighteenth-century France. They also made a revolutionary proclamation of the principles of a new golden age. But, while the Declaration proclaimed the universality of rights and the civic equality of all citizens, it was ambiguous on whether those without significant property would have political as well as legal equality, and was silent on how the means to exercise one's talents could be secured by those without the education or property necessary to do so. With the Assembly's prevarication on the full abolition of seigneurial dues, these ambiguities and silences were to underpin ongoing uncertainty and confrontation in rural France. The insistence of rural communities that the seigneurial system be totally abolished, which was realised in 1792–3, and their search for full political and civic equality, only temporarily achieved at the same time, drove the Revolution in directions which could not have been anticipated in 1789 and which underpin the status of the Revolution as a turning point in social history.

Notes

Parts of this article draw (with permission from Palgrave Macmillan) from Peter McPhee, *Living the French Revolution 1789–1799* (London, 2006).

1. Georges Lefebvre, *Les Paysans du Nord pendant la Révolution française* (Bari, 1959); 'La place de la Révolution dans l'histoire agraire de la France', *Annales d'histoire économique et sociale*, 1 (1929), pp.506–23; 'La Révolution française et les paysans', *Annales historiques de la Révolution française* [hereafter *AHRF*], 10 (1933), pp.97–128.
2. Alfred Cobban, *The Social Interpretation of the French Revolution* (Cambridge, 1964). Note, for example, the collection edited and introduced by Peter R. Campbell, *The Origins of the French Revolution* (Houndmills and New York, 2006), in which John Markoff's contribution on the peasantry sits awkwardly alongside political and cultural history.
3. David Andress, *The French Revolution and the People* (London and New York, 2004), p.103.
4. D.M.G. Sutherland, *The French Revolution and Empire: the Quest for a Civic Order* (Oxford, 2003), p.387.
5. P.M. Jones, *The Peasantry in the French Revolution* (Cambridge, 1988); *Liberty and Locality in Revolutionary France: Six Villages Compared, 1760–1820* (Cambridge, 2003); Gilbert Shapiro and John Markoff, *Revolutionary Demands: a Content Analysis of the Cahiers de Doléances of 1789* (Stanford, CA, 1998); John Markoff, *The Abolition of Feudalism: Peasants, Lords, and Legislators in the French Revolution* (University Park, PA, 1996); Serge Bianchi, *La Révolution et la première république au village. Pouvoirs, votes et politisation dans les campagnes d'Île-de-France 1787–1800* (Paris, 2004); Jean Boutier, *Campagnes en émoi. Révoltes et Révolution en Bas-Limousin, 1789–1800* (Treignac, 1987); Jean-Pierre Jessenne, *Pouvoir au village et revolution: Artois, 1760–1848* (Lille, 1987).
6. Guy Lemarchand, '*La féodalité et la Révolution française: seigneurie et communauté paysanne (1780–1799)*', *AHRF*, 242 (1980), pp.536–58; '*Troubles populaires au XVIIIe siècle et conscience de classe: une préface à la Révolution française*', *AHRF*, 279 (1990), pp.32–48; Jones, *Peasantry*, pp.53–8; Jean Nicolas, *La rébellion française: mouvements populaires et conscience sociale 1661–1789* (Paris, 2002).
7. James C. Scott, *Weapons of the Weak: Everyday Forms of Peasant Resistance* (New Haven, CT, 1985); *Domination and the Arts of Resistance: Hidden Transcripts* (New Haven, CT, 1990).
8. The analysis which follows is based on several thousand parish *cahiers* which were published in the first half of the twentieth century under the auspices of the Ministère de l'Instruction Publique as the *Collection de documents inédits sur l'histoire économique de la Révolution française*. This series is outlined in Shapiro and Markoff, *Revolutionary Demands*, pp.117–19.
9. Note the comments on this issue by Shapiro and Markoff, *Revolutionary Demands*, pp.140–7; Jones, *Peasantry*, pp.58–67; Markoff, *The Abolition of Feudalism*,

pp.25–9.
10. *Cahiers de doléances du bailliage d'Amont*, vol.1 (Besançon, 1918); vol.2 (Auxerre, 1927).
11. Gilbert Larguier et al. (eds), *Cahiers de doléances audios* (Carcassonne, 1989); Peter McPhee, *Revolution and Environment in Southern France: Peasant, Lords, and Murder in the Corbières, 1780–1830* (Oxford, 1999), p.42.
12. Edward A. Allen, 'L'influence des cahiers modèles en 1789: l'expérience du Gard', *AHRF*, 291 (1993), pp.13–31.
13. Larguier et al. (eds), *Cahiers audois*, pp.20–1, Annexes IV and V. See the comments of Shapiro and Markoff, *Revolutionary Demands*, pp.147–60. An insightful methodological reflection is by Vivian R. Gruder, 'Can we hear the voices of peasants? France, 1788', *History of European Ideas*, 17 (1993), pp.167–90.
14. Philip Dawson (ed.), *The French Revolution* (Englewood Cliffs, NJ, 1967), pp.16–18, 30–2.
15. *La Révolution vue de l'Aisne, en 200 documents* (Laon, 1990), p.18.
16. Gilbert Larguier et al., 'Les assemblées primaires de la sénéchaussée de Carcassonne (8–16 mars 1789): typologie et composition sociale,' *Bulletin de la Société des Etudes Scientifiques de l'Aude*, 89 (1989), pp.101–20. See also Shapiro and Markoff, *Revolutionary Demands*, pp.136–40.
17. McPhee, *Revolution and Environment*, ch.1.
18. Jones, *Peasantry*, ch.2; D.M.G. Sutherland, *The Chouans: The Social Origins of Popular Counter-Revolution in Upper Brittany, 1770–1796* (Oxford, 1982), p.70; 'Peasants, lords, and leviathan: winners and losers from the abolition of French feudalism, 1780–1820', *Journal of Economic History*, 62 (2002), pp.1–24.
19. Markoff, *The Abolition of Feudalism*; Shapiro and Markoff, *Revolutionary Demands*.
20. Denise, Maurice and Robert Bréant, *Menucourt. Un village du Vexin français pendant la Révolution 1789–1799* (Menucourt, 1989), pp.45–6.
21. See, for example, Colin Jones, *The Great Nation: France from Louis XV to Napoleon* (New York, 2002); Hilton L. Root, *Peasant and King in Burgundy: Agrarian Foundations of French Absolutism* (Berkeley, CA, 1987); David Bell, *Lawyers and Citizens: the Making of a Political Elite in Old Regime France* (New York, 1994).
22. Nicole Castan, *Justice et répression en Languedoc* (Paris, 1980), pp.54–82; Jeremy D. Hayhoe, 'Neighbours before the court: crime, village communities and seigneurial justice in northern Burgundy, 1750–1790', *French History*, 17 (2003), pp.127–48; Sutherland, *The Chouans*, pp.182–4; Jonathan Dewald, *Pont-St.-Pierre, 1378–1789: Lordship, Community and Capitalism in Early Modern France* (Berkeley and Los Angeles, 1987), pp.254–5; Steven G. Reinhardt, *Justice in the Sarladais, 1770–1790* (Baton Rouge, 1991).
23. Markoff, *The Abolition of Feudalism*, p.116.
24. Anthony Crubaugh, *Balancing the Scales of Justice. Local Courts and Rural Society in Southwest France, 1750–1800* (University Park, PA, 2001). Cf. William Doyle, 'Was there an aristocratic reaction in pre-revolutionary France?', *Past and Present*,

57 (1972), pp.97–122; Guy Lemarchand, *Féodalisme, société et Révolution française: études d'histoire moderne, xvie–xviiie siècles* (Caen, 2000); Jones, *Peasantry*, pp.53–8.
25. Jones, *Peasantry*, pp.94–8.
26. Shapiro and Markoff, *Revolutionary Demands*, esp. ch.14 and Appendix I; Markoff, *The Abolition of Feudalism*.
27. In general on anti-industrial grievances in the *cahiers*, see Andrée Corvol, *L'homme aux bois. Histoire des relations de l'homme et de la forêt, XVIIe–XXe siècle* (Paris, 1987), pp.71–8. A fascinating account of one mine and its antagonists is by Gwynne Lewis, *The Advent of Modern Capitalism in France 1770–1840: The Contribution of Pierre-François Tubeuf* (Oxford, 1993).
28. *Cahiers de doléances des bailliages des généralités de Metz et de Nancy pour les Etats-Généraux de 1789*, vol.1 (Nancy, 1907), pp.13, 43. See Jean-Pierre Husson, 'Les paysages forestiers lorrains, rôle et impact de l'épisode révolutionnaire (étude de géographie historique)', in Denis Woronoff (ed.), *Révolution et espaces forestiers* (Paris, 1988), pp.63–70.
29. *Cahiers de doléances des bailliages des généralités de Metz et de Nancy pour les Etats-Généraux de 1789*, pp.130–1.
30 *Cahiers de doléances des bailliages des généralités de Metz et de Nancy pour les Etats-Généraux de 1789*, p.175.
31. Alain Le Bloas, 'La question du domaine congéable', *AHRF*, 331 (2003), pp.1–27.
32. *Cahiers de doléances des sénéchaussées de Quimper et de Concarneau pour les Etats-Généraux de 1789*, 100; *Cahiers de doléances de la sénéchaussée de Rennes pour les Etats-Généraux de 1789*, vol.4, p.152 (Ploumogoar).
33. *Cahiers de doléances du bailliage de Troyes et du bailliage de Bar-sur-Seine pour les Etats-Généraux de 1789*, vol.2, p.32.
34. *Cahiers de doléances du bailliage de Mirecourt*, p.133.
35. Corvol, *L'Homme aux bois*, ch.8.
36. *Cahiers de doléances pour les Etats-Généraux de 1789: Département de la Marne*, vol.1, p.642.
37. *Cahiers de doléances des bailliages des généralités de Metz et de Nancy pour les Etats-Généraux de 1789*, vol.1, p.639.
38. *Cahiers de doléances des bailliages des généralités de Metz et de Nancy pour les Etats-Généraux de 1789*, vol.3, p.142.
39. Jacques Bernet (ed.), *Le journal d'un maître d'école d'Île-de-France (1771–1792): Silly-en-Multien de l'Ancien Régime à la Révolution* (Villeneuve-d'Asq, 2000), pp.181–3. The commune is today Silly-le-Long.
40. *Cahiers de doléances du bailliage d'Amont*, vol.2, 199. I owe this reference to Kieko Matteson.
41. Etienne Frénay (ed.), *Cahiers de doléances de la province de Roussillon (1789)* (Perpignan, 1979), pp.163–4.
42. Anatoli Ado, *Paysans en Révolution. Terre, pouvoir et jacquerie 1789–1794*. Translated by Serge Aberdam, Marcel Dorigny et al. (Paris, 1996), p.114.
43. Frénay (ed.), *Cahiers de doléances de la province de Roussillon*; Larguier et al. (eds),

Cahiers de doléances audois; McPhee, *Revolution and Environment*, p.42.
44. McPhee, *Revolution and Environment*, p.47.
45. McPhee, *Revolution and Environment*, p.60.
46. See Peter McPhee, 'Frontiers, ethnicity and identity in the French Revolution: Catalans and Occitans', in Ian Coller, Helen Davies and Julie Kalman (eds), *French History and Civilization: Papers from the George Rudé Seminar*, 1 (2005), pp.30–7. Also at http://www.h-france.net/rude/rudeTOC2005.html. Note the comments on 'localism' by Markoff, *The Abolition of Feudalism*, p.137*n*.
47. Markoff, *The Abolition of Feudalism*, p.226.
48. Jean Boutier, 'Jacqueries en pays croquant: les révoltes paysannes en Aquitaine (décembre 1789–mars 1790)', *AHRF*, 34 (1979), p.765. See, also, Boutier's *Campagnes en émoi* for the endemic violence in the Bas-Limousin region.
49. Nicole Castan, *Les criminels du Languedoc: les exigences d'ordre et les voies du ressentiment dans une société pré-Révolutionnaire (1750–1790)* (Toulouse, 1980), p.159 and chs 3–4; Yves Castan, *Honnêteté et relations sociales en Languedoc, 1715–1780* (Paris, 1974); Olwen Hufton, 'Attitudes towards authority in eighteenth-century Languedoc', *Social History* 3 (1978), pp.281–302; Georges Fournier, *Démocratie et vie municipale en Languedoc du milieu du XVIIIe au début du XIXe siècle*, 2 vols (Toulouse, 1994); Jean-Claude Nicod, 'Les "séditieux" en Languedoc à la fin du XVIIIe siècle', *Recueil de Mémoires et travaux de la Société d'histoire du droit et des institutions des anciens pays de droit écrit*, 8 (1971), pp.145–65; McPhee, *Revolution and Environment*, pp.36–9.
50. On this point see Jones, *Liberty and Locality in Revolutionary France*, ch.3 and pp.266–7.
51. On the elections of 1789, see Malcolm Crook, *Elections in the French Revolution: An Apprenticeship in Democracy, 1789–1799* (Cambridge and New York, 1996), ch.1; Jones, *Peasantry*, pp.28, 62–4.
52. Jones, *Peasantry*, pp.65–7; Georges Lefevbre, *The Great Fear of 1789: Rural Panic in Revolutionary France* [1932], Joan White (trans) (New York, 1973), p.39.
53. Eugène Dubois, *Histoire de la Révolution dans l'Ain*, vol.1, *La Constituante (1789–1791)* (Bourg, 1931), pp.60–8; Louis Trenard, 'Le "vandalisme révolutionnaire" dans les pays de l'Ain: faits matériels et motivations', in Simone Bernard-Griffiths, Marie-Claude Chemin and Jean Ehrard, *Révolution française et 'vandalisme révolutionnaire'. Actes du colloque international de Clermont-Ferrand 15–17 décembre 1988* (Paris, 1992), pp.252–3.
54. Bernet (ed.), *Le journal d'un maître d'école*, pp.189, 195–6.
55. Claude Muller, 'Religion et Révolution en Alsace', *AHRF*, 337 (2004), p.70; Timothy Tackett, 'Collective panics in the early French Revolution', *French History*, 17 (2003), pp.149–58.
56. Christian Bonnet, 'Les pillages d'abbayes dans le Nord et leur signification (1789–1793)', in Bernard-Griffiths, Chemin and Ehrard, *Révolution française et 'vandalisme révolutionnaire'*, pp.169–73.
57. This tactic was brilliantly studied by George Rudé, *The Crowd in History* (New York, 1964).

58. *AHRF*, 1955, pp.161–2.
59. Clay Ramsay, *The Ideology of the Great Fear: The Soissonnais in 1789* (Baltimore, MD and London, 1992), ch.8.
60. On this point, see Peter McPhee, '"The misguided greed of peasants"? Popular attitudes to the environment in the Revolution of 1789', *French Historical Studies*, 24 (2001), pp.247–69.
61. Markoff, *The Abolition of Feudalism*, p.5. Note, too, the reflections of Melvin Edelstein, 'La place de la Révolution française dans la politisation des paysans', *AHRF*, 280 (1993), pp.135–44; and Colin Lucas, 'Aux sources du comportement politique de la paysannerie beaujolaise', in *La Révolution française et le monde rural. Actes du colloque tenu en Sorbonne les 23, 24 et 25 octobre 1987* (Paris, 1989), pp.345–65.
62. William Doyle, *Origins of the French Revolution*, 2nd edn (Oxford, 1980), p.198; Markoff, *The Abolition of Feudalism*, p.72.
63. Michael P. Fitzsimmons, *The Night the Old Regime Ended: August 4, 1789 and the French Revolution* (University Park, PA, 2003); Jones, *Peasantry*, pp.81–5; Markoff, *The Abolition of Feudalism*, ch.8.

Perspectives

Forum on 1688
Institute of Historical Research, 23 May 2007
Steve Pincus, John Callow and Bill Speck

The Revolution of 1688–9 in England was the first modern revolution: it radically transformed the English state and society. The Revolution had long-term causes and long-term consequences. It was popular. It was violent. And, like all modern revolutions, it was divisive. The Revolution transformed, and was intended to transform, England's relations with Europe and with the wider world. The revolutionaries also radically transformed the Church of England and the economic policies of the regime. England's Revolution of 1688–9, like all modern revolutions, was not a conflict between a modernising faction or class against an entrenched *ancien regime*. Instead, the Revolution of 1688–9 was a bitter conflict between groups espousing competing models of modernity. Both Jacobites and Williamites were modernisers. In this sense as well the Revolution of 1688–9 had a great deal in common with the French, American, Russian, Mexican, Iranian, Chinese, and Cuban revolutions.

Many in the eighteenth century understood the Revolution of 1688–9 as a fundamental turning point in history. On 30 November 1789, just after the outbreak of the French Revolution, one Monsieur Navier stood up to address the Patriotic Society of Dijon, the chief city of Burgundy. 'Why should we be ashamed, Gentleman,' he asked his auditors, 'to acknowledge that the Revolution which is now establishing itself in our country, is owing to the example given by England a century ago? It was from that day we became acquainted with the political constitution of that island, and the prosperity with which it was accompanied; it was from that day our hatred of despotism derived its energy. In securing their own happiness, Englishmen have prepared the way for that of the universe.' These sentiments were widespread in France in the second half of the eighteenth century. Many in the British Isles, too, understood the Revolution of 1688–9 as a great climacteric. They saw the Revolution as inaugurating a new age of liberty. 'From the era of the revolution,' argued the Scottish light John Millar, 'we may trace…a new order of things.'[1] This was not merely a Scottish view. 'Since the Revolution in eighty-eight,' declared the former ambassador Robert Molesworth in 1711, 'we stand upon another and better bottom.'[2]

Many eighteenth-century commentators understood the Revolution of 1688–9 as much more than a mere political or constitutional revolution. Opposition Whigs and their ideological fellow travellers emphasised that the Revolution transformed the political economy of Britain. 'The full establishment of a regular and free constitution,' establishing 'the secure possession and enjoyment of property,' was, in John Millar's view, 'obtained by the memorable Revolution in 1688,' ensuring that 'commerce and manufactures assumed a new aspect.'[3]

The revolutionaries of 1688–9 provided one modern model for taking advantage of profound social and economic changes that had taken place since 1640. These changes were both the necessary preconditions of revolution and the necessary preconditions for the modern French-style state constructed by Charles II and James II. While I provide a range of documentary evidence to elaborate these changes in my book manuscript, my conclusions follow the footsteps of the eighteenth-century commentators. David Hume, for example, emphasised that 'the commerce and riches of England did never during any period increase so fast as from the restoration to the revolution.'[4] William Blackstone pointed to the development of the post office, the proliferation of hackney coaches, the 'discovery of the Indies', the advancement of learning as paving the way for the great climacteric of 1688. 'The great revolutions that had happened in manners and in property,' he noted, 'had paved the way, by imperceptible yet sure degrees, for as great a revolution in government.' Yet, Blackstone was careful to note, 'while that revolution was effecting, the crown became more arbitrary than ever, by the progress of these very means which afterwards reduced its power.'[5] Many Opposition Whigs and their fellow travellers in the eighteenth century understood the Revolution of 1688–9 as the first modern revolution, not only because it established political liberty but also because it transformed the nature of English society.

Of course, no modern scholar claims that the Revolution of 1688–9 was the first modern revolution. 'British history,' observes the American social scientist Charles Tilly, 'now provides a much-thumbed manual for the avoidance of revolution.'⁶ The image of English stability, inevitably contrasted with French volatility, has now been long in the making. Recent scholarly work on the later seventeenth century has tended to reinforce that view. In fact, from the 1720s this has been the establishment, Whig interpretation of the events of 1688–9. The revolution of 1688–9 was a necessary adjustment, a sensible revolution, a political but not a social revolution, a British revolution. For Burke, Macaulay, Trevelyan (and for more recent scholars), the un-revolutionary revolution of 1688–9 confirmed the distinctiveness, the exceptionalist nature of British history. It was the hegemony of this interpretation that guaranteed that the Tercentenary of the Revolution would pass largely unnoticed. No wonder the leader of the House of Lords, Viscount Whitelaw, could assert confidently that there was no 'general wish' for a lavish celebration of the Revolution of 1688–9.[7] The Glorious Revolution, opined Patricia Morrison in the *Daily Telegraph*, had 'little box office appeal'.[8]

Scholars have seen the Revolution of 1688–9 as an un-revolutionary revolution because they have been asking the wrong questions. They have asked why was James II overthrown in 1688–9 not why and how was England transformed after 1688–9. Scholarship on the Revolution has suffered from two fatal flaws. First, it has assumed that the fall of James II was a high political event with short-term causes and short-term consequences. Scholarship on the Revolution of 1688–9 has followed the Tory inclination of the 1690s in seeking its origins in the reign of James II, and declaring the Revolution to have ended with Treaty of Limerick of 1691. But, this is not the way that scholars who work on revolutions conceptualise them. The rapidity of revolutions must be measured in years not in months. 'Revolutions', as the sociologist of revolutions Jeff Goodwin has pointed out, 'are best conceptualised not as events, but as processes that typically span many years or even decades.'[9] The Russian Revolution, in Sheila Fitzpatrick's view lasted through Stalin's purges. The events of October 1917, by themselves, she suggests were a coup. Alan Knight's work on the Mexican Revolution covers several decades. Much work on the French Revolution—including François Furet's—demands an even longer time frame. Would the French revolution have seemed such a transformative event if historical accounts ended with the recalling of the Estates General or the Fall of the Bastille? Would the American Revolution be considered a radical event if one focused on the years 1774–8?

Second, the scholarship on the Revolution of 1688–9 has been remarkably insular. It has been rigorously uncomparative. Scholars have been happy to proclaim English peculiarity without having read deeply in European history or in the history of other revolutions. Thus, the assumption that there were no social and economic causes or contexts for the revolution—a claim central to the historiography of 1688–9 ever since the publication of Thomas Babington Macaulay's wonderful and evocative chapter 3—fails to take into account scholarship that has demonstrated that English society and economy diverged from the continental pattern in the period between 1640–1700. Scholarship insisting that party conflict in later seventeent-century England was un-modern, has ignored almost a generation of new work in political science that has radically redefined the nature of modern political parties. Nor has any attempt been made to compare the English Catholicism of James II's court with the varieties of continental Catholicism.

So, why do I think the Revolution of 1688–9 was the first modern revolution? I think the Revolution of 1688–9 fundamentally transformed the trajectory of English, European and world history. Charles II and especially James II were in the process of harnessing England's newly dynamic economy to create a sophisticated modern state, with a modern army and navy, with an ever-growing and ideologically committed state bureaucracy. James II, in particular, had developed modern technologies to stifle political dissent—utilising the expanded post office to promote surveillance, conducting political surveys, and manipulating the rewards of local office. All of this, it must be emphasised was very much modelled on the self-consciously modern state apparatus developed by Louis XIV.

The Williamite state, by contrast, was equally modern but very different in ideological orientation. That post-revolutionary state was a strong state. It was a state also able to support a modern navy, but it was a state that did so using a different set of financial techniques, a different taxation scheme, and with a different model of political participation. That model did draw very heavily on the Dutch. But that model did not come to England with William in 1689 but had been actively advocated by English radicals beginning in the 1650s.

The revolutionaries of 1688–9 fundamentally transformed England in three areas. First, there was a transformation in foreign and imperial policy. James II's regime had a decidedly anti-Dutch orientation. James and his advisors despised Dutch republicanism as a political cancer, they disliked Dutch political culture for its amoral behaviour, and they feared Dutch support for England's rebels. England's future, James and his advisors, calculated, lay in seizing control of the Indies and the Americas from the Dutch. The post-revolutionary regime, pushed forward by a deeply and passionately Francophobic public opinion, declared war on France. France, they argued, sought universal monarchy, insisted on depriving European and extra-European states of the liberty of choosing their own governments, and harboured England's exiled Stuarts. There was, however, no post-revolutionary consensus. From the first Tories argued that England should not be engaged in a continental war. England's interests were narrowly British and Atlantic. They should fight France exclusively on the seas. Whigs, by contrast, argued that France could only be stopped by engaging on the continent and by aligning with other European powers.

Second, there was a revolutionary transformation of the Church of England. From the 1670s the highest posts in the Church of England were filled by a group of clerics who came to be known as high churchmen. They were committed to a narrow and intolerant church, to the notion that no resistance against legitimate sovereigns was religiously justifiable, and to a form of pastoral care that insisted that no social relief should be administered to non-communicants in the church. Between 1689 and 1692, the new monarchs William and Mary had the opportunity to fill eighteen episcopal vacancies. The men they selected were almost uniformly from the low church party. They argued for a broader church that was simultaneously more tolerant of religious practice outside the church, the possibility of secular justifications for resistance to political tyranny (they agreed with the high churchmen that religion could never justify political resistance), and for a pastoral care that insisted minimal social needs must be met before issues of religious observance could be raised. Starving men made bad Christians, they often said.

Finally, there was a revolution in political economy. The Revolution of 1688–9 dramatically reoriented England's social and economic policy. James, and his advisors believed that the basis of all property and wealth was land. It was land that provided the agrarian base for all economies. Since the amount of land in the world was necessarily finite, the struggle for prosperity was a zero-sum game—what one nation gained, another lost. James, therefore, sought to rationalise and promote England's imperial possessions. In North America James, while still Duke of York, amalgamated New York, Rhode Island, Connecticut, and Massachusetts to create the Dominion of New England in 1684. He sought to create a parallel Dominion of the West Indies. And he began to create a new Dominion of India based in Bombay. Because James assumed the viciousness of international competition, the English monarch worked with the African and East India Companies, as well as his Board of Trade, to ensure that these colonies would be militarily self-sufficient.

James II's economic policy had clear domestic corollaries as well. Since land, and not manufacturing, was the basis of wealth, James sought to promote England's landed gentlemen at the expense of the newly developing manufacturing sectors. Land was lightly taxed, whereas the hearth tax imposed after Charles II's restoration heavily assessed those who needed heat to manufacture their products. Sheffield metal workers, for example, deeply resented the tax policies of the later Stuart monarchs.

James II and his friends did not, however, hold a monopoly on economic ideas in the later seventeenth century. Their ideas were opposed by another powerful, wealthy, and influential group of merchants. Many of these merchants had been purged from the East India Company in the 1670s and 1680s, and many had ties to England's manufacturing community or were themselves manufacturers. Unlike the circle around James II, they argued that the basis of property and wealth was human labour rather than land. Since wealth was created by work, it was not necessarily finite; it was infinitely expandable. As a result, economic competition was not a zero-sum game; it was possible for several nations to become wealthier simultaneously. Within each kingdom manufacturing would drive the national economy. As workers produced more, they would have more disposable income with which to purchase more goods, in turn stimulating more industries. In this view there were no limits to economic growth.

From these assumptions grew an alternative understanding of economic and imperial policy. Proponents of this view argued that the key to England's long-term prosperity was in manufacturing. Therefore the East India trade, a trade that imported finished calicoes and other cheap cloths that competed with the English clothing industry, should be discouraged. The West Indies, by contrast, which produced sugar to be refined in England and tobacco that could be re-exported throughout Europe was another matter. Similarly, proponents of this view understood the international economic order very differently. Since, in their view, trade was infinitely expandable, these merchants did not see Dutch economic prosperity as threatening. The French, by contrast, were a danger. French protectionist policies excluded English manufactures from French markets. And, the diplomatic pressure the French were able to exert on other countries closed even more markets to the English. Unsurprisingly many of the loudest proponents of this view were merchants who once traded heavily with France.

On the domestic front, proponents of this view shared with their opponents the conviction that the state should intervene in the economy. But, unlike James II and his supporters, those who thought that wealth was infinitely expandable argued that government economic policy should favour the manufacturing sector rather than the landed élite. They hated the hearth tax for harming manufacturers and longed for a return to the high land taxes of the 1640s and 1650s.

After William and Mary succeeded in overthrowing James II, the defenders of England's manufacturing sector gained the upper hand. The same Parliament that placed William on the throne reversed James II's taxation policies. In 1689 the hearth tax was repealed and a land tax was instituted for the first time since the 1650s. Many then turned their attention to the monopoly held by the East India Company. In session after session of Parliament in the 1690s proposals were put forward to disband or reorganize the East India Company. While the company's opponents succeeded in establishing the principle that all companies were subject to Parliament and English law, the company itself remained. It survived in large part because in a time of warfare against the French, the East India Company had the potential to offer the government large loans to pay for an increasingly expensive war. The company's opponents, however, merely shifted their ground. They succeeded in limiting the East India Company's influence by establishing the Bank of England in 1694 that simultaneously loaned the government money to pay for the war and helped redistribute money in the form of loans to the manufacturing sector. The Bank, supported politically by James II's opponents such as John Locke and Isaac Newton and financially by the old enemies of the East India company, was based on the notion that England's economic future lay in the manufacturing sector and not exclusively in the land.

By the late 1690s—certainly in the aftermath of the assassination plot of 1696—it was clear to both the regime's supporters and its detractors that a radical revolution had been begun by 1688–9. Was there radical transformation without revolutionary activity? Was 1688–9 an aristocratic and bloodless revolution? Extensive archival research suggests that the revolution was in fact both popular and extremely violent. Scholars have significantly underestimated the extent of English popular involvement in the Revolution. Thousands took up arms in support of William. There were popular risings throughout England—as well as in Scotland and parts of Ireland. Many Englishmen went into exile to join William's invasion force. Still others contributed financially to the overthrow of James's regime. While many aristocrats did play a significant role in these activities, the masses who took arms should not be understood as taking part in a baronial revolt. Crowd activity in 1688–9 was remarkably similar to that in other revolutions. 'Revolutions', Crane Brinton has reminded us, 'are not begun by the poor and downtrodden.'[10] In England as in France a century later popular elements worked in co-ordination with the higher orders. In part because of the extensive popular activity in 1688–9, the Revolution was far from bloodless. There was extensive mob violence throughout England in late 1688, violence that terrified local populations and resulted in extensive damage to property and individuals. It is true that the expected civil war never occurred in England because of the rapid collapse of James's army. Instead James chose to conduct his war in Scotland and Ireland, conflicts that need to be seen as part of the bloody Nine Years War.

The Revolution of 1688–9 was the first modern revolution. It transformed the English state in radical ways to be sure. But it also transformed English society—those who pursued an economic agenda favouring manufacturing as opposed to a traditional understanding of an agrarian economy gained the upper hand. The failure of the Land Bank in 1696 and the ultimate triumph of the Bank of England was both symbol and artefact of that revolutionary transformation. It would be wrong, however, to see the revolutionaries as the only defenders of modernity. James and his supporters also saw the late seventeenth century as a turning point for England. They, however, had modelled their version of modernity on that of Louis XIV's France, while the revolutionaries had long looked to the Netherlands for inspiration. The struggle in 1688–9 was not between tradition and modernity but between two competing models of modernity.

John Callow

Some of the points Steve has mentioned are going to find a little echo in this, because I guess in some ways we are travelling over similar ground. What I am going to talk to you about is a little bit about the way the revolution is being conceptualised. Why in lots of ways it seems to us to be a revolution that never was. I can remember when I started out on post-graduate work going through the index of theses there seemed to be inches worth of material being raked over the Civil War. Once you got into the 1680s, let alone the 1690s, let alone Queen Anne there was hardly anything. So that is one reason why I thought it was an interesting area.

If bewilderment was the key emotion experienced by the followers of James II, when he disappeared overnight on the 23 December 1688 leaving the Tories leaderless and explicitly forbidden from forming a party by repeated injunctions for them to sit tight and to wait upon events, then Prince William and his Whig allies might have been forgiven for exuding a quiet sense of triumph, as they prepared to step into, and to fill, the political vacuum left by the king's sudden, and fortuitous second flight. His departure appeared to confirm the authority of the lords who sat in the Guildhall to act as if they were the *de facto* government, and to justify their attempts to negotiate a hasty redrawing of the constitution with William of Orange.

In the absence of James, it was far easier to countenance the view that the 'Stupendous Revolution', to use a contemporary term, that had struck at his person and policies had, in fact, been nothing of the sort and that the king had openly acknowledged his incapacity for office by his desertion of his Crown and his lands. Herein lay both the formula that allowed many different, and frequently conflicting, interest groups to coalesce and achieve a truly revolutionary constitutional settlement, as has been said, written over years rather than days and months, while maintaining—with a fairly good conscience—that it was nothing of the kind; and also the germ of the idea, which has become popular in recent years, that the king had been pushed out of England by unrepresentative conservative forces, within the establishment, and by the decisive use of foreign arms. In this version of events, and I shall say a little bit later about why this has been allowed to persist for so long, James can be turned into a thoroughly modern figure: the patriot, the warrior and forward thinking champion of religious and cultural plurality. It is a vision I'd suggest every bit as attuned to the concerns and paradigms of our own uncertain times, as was the mid-nineteenth century image of James in exile, as the unheeded prophet of empire, the embodiment of gentlemanly virtues. This is the image found in Harrison Ainsworth's three-volume novel on James II where he appears as a wonderful Victorian gentleman who brings boy and girl together in the last act. Everybody goes off happily and he is left to potter about in his garden. That is one of the Victorian ideas and it certainly captured one significant corner of the Victorian imagination.[11] However, it is no less flawed for all that, and lies rooted, not in the tumults of 1688–9 or in the refashioning of James's political legacy during the years of his final exile, but in the collapse of the monumental edifice that was the Whig school of history and in the reduction of the events following James II's fall from power, in much recent scholarship, to just a sad and tarnished spectacle of the revolution that never was.

What I would also just like to signal here is that this has been allowed to happen effectively because there was no left-wing rejoinder. The left never managed, in its heyday, to conceptualise or put forward an attractive vision of the revolution. It's too mired in what later happened in Ireland. In fact one of the few bits of good popular radical literature is a little story called *Drums and Trumpets* by Geoffrey Trease, the children's author. He makes no bones about it being a revolution. His book never got reprinted and one of the reasons for that is the very negative portrayal of the Irish soldiers camped on Salisbury Plain. Trease wrote the book in India, missing home, and had Churchill's marvellous life of Marlborough to hand as source material.

The grand sweeps of historical narrative, as we have already heard from

Steve, pioneered brilliantly by Macaulay and Trevelyan, gripping, incisive and opinionated, compelling in style and scope, held few doubts as to either the beneficial effects of James II's removal from the throne or his harsh and destructive brand of bigotry that encapsulated the man. For them the Glorious Revolution had led naturally and necessarily to the sovereignty of Parliament, the establishment of the Bank of England, to an aggressive colonial policy and to the intellectual syntheses of John Locke and Sir Isaac Newton. Following on from which we have the Industrial Revolution and the supremacy of the British Empire. It unfolds like a tapestry and seems to have grown inevitably from the freedoms won in 1688–9, and consolidated in the following years when it became possible to cast James as an effective foil for William of Orange. For, where William was brave, rational and thoroughly adaptable to events, in the Whig view, James could be seen as cowardly, illogical and curiously rigid, a king who had fortuitously disappeared from the political stage, into a long and disagreeable political exile, before he could do too much damage to either people or state—a rather comforting picture, overlooking the last decade of his political career.

Yet for Britons today, grappling their way through an uncertain political terrain of the early twenty-first century, such confidence in economic, social and scientific progress, or in the perfection of a constitution that remains unwritten—what Gordon Brown is trying to get his head round—might appear to be hopeful at best and, at the very worst, the very stuff of an irrelevant and dated Whig mythology that bears little scrutiny. The upheavals of 1688–9 can no longer be seen to provide the decisive point in a continuing ascent to commercial prosperity and political dominance. Britannia clearly no longer rules the waves, the bonds of the nation state have creaked under devolution, and the parliament at Westminster, sidelined—at the moment—by a more presidential style of government can no longer be perceived as the model for an effective administration that might be made general and applied throughout an envious world. As Steve suggested the last flickering of the Whig tradition could be discerned in the decidedly lacklustre tercentenary celebrations held in 1988, at the Banqueting Hall in Whitehall, to mark 'the moment when the balance of power finally shifted from the Crown to Parliament'.[12] In contrast to the large, and genuinely popular, celebrations held in the Netherlands and the United States, the talking mannequins of William and Mary—in those days thought quite 'high tech'—installed in Whitehall at enormous public cost, appear to have inspired little interest among London's tourists, while thick rolling fog conspired to thoroughly obscure the visit of Queen Elizabeth II and the Duke of Edinburgh, onboard the royal yacht, to Brixham harbour.[13] Although the members of the Tercentenary Trust, the government quango charged with organising the commemorations, had correctly defined the period as representing something of a 'black hole in the school curriculum' they had done little to remedy matters in the classroom. Worse still, they were singularly unwilling to address the central problem threatening the celebrations: that of the appropriation of the image of William of Orange, as Protestant champion, by hard-line Ulster politicians. Elsewhere in the United Kingdom, save for a handful of football grounds, confessional conflict had retreated to the far-flung fringes of society, while the religious passions that had cost James II his throne appeared wholly strange and inexplicable to the vast majority of the inhabitants of these increasingly secular times. However, in the North of Ireland, where troops still patrolled the streets, Unionist and Republican para-militaries drilled and clashed by night, and where the variations in accent marked the sharp demarcation lines between Protestant and Catholic communities, the language and the controversies of the seventeenth century were still very much alive in a bitterly contested and still divided land. The understandable concern not to be seen as condoning the later establishment of the Protestant ascendancy and the operation of the Penal Laws, carried ironically against the will of King William himself, undoubtedly served, in part, to explain the willingness of members of the Old Left to unite with the torchbearers of the New Right in a visceral attack upon the supposed aims and objectives of the Revolution, and all that it stood for.[14] Yet, it was the protracted failure of the Left, I would argue, to examine the events of 1688–9 for what they were, rather than for what they had wished they had been, that permitted this unedifying alliance and allowed the gradual resurgence of a potent Tory historiography, that threatened to first divorce the 'Glory' from the Revolution, and then to deny the existence of any sort of revolution at all.

There was palpable disappointment in the lament of Christopher Hill, the great seventeenth century Marxist historian, when he said, 'James II ran away too easily in 1688'. In running away he failed to ignite a popular revolution, or to fan the embers of a new and radicalising civil war.[15] Of course historians love warfare, excitement, revolutionary turmoil: but I think if you were sitting in Newcastle on the dock side in 1688, or walking across London Bridge keeping an eye on the army in Blackheath, or still skulking in Somerset after the Bloody Assizes you might have been quiet glad that there was not a civil war. Defoe grew up in revolutionary Colchester and his *Tour of Britain* still bears the scars of the siege of Colchester that he had heard about from the generation above him. For the most part, those Marxist historians who chose to follow in Hill's mighty shadow preferred to focus both scholarly and popular attention upon the English Revolution of 1640–49, downplaying the significance of the Glorious Revolution and relegating it to the outer realms of a rather dour form of economic determinism. This had not always been the case. At the high-water mark of socialist self-confidence following the Second World War, the Revolution of 1688–9 was, celebrated in the form of giant floods at a pageant of working-class history held at the Royal Albert Hall.[16] However, all this had changed by the late 1980s, when Lawrence and Wishart, the radical publishers sponsored a conference whose title was—remember the American films of the time—'Back to the Future'. This was not, maybe, the best way to refashion Marxism for a new generation. It reflected the fundamental malaise and crisis of identity that had begun to grip certain sections of the Left. Despite coinciding with the official commemorations organised by the Tercentenary Trust, the conference virtually ignored the themes surrounding the Glorious Revolution and invited Jonathan Clark, one of the most impressive of the rising generation of right-wing, revisionist scholars, to give a keynote address. They could not find any one to put up against him to give a good show or who wouldn't have been eaten alive by him! Perhaps Bill was out of the country, or he didn't get the call! We all make mistakes. Clark had already rejected the 'precarious' notion of the significance of James II's fall altogether, citing the persistence of Jacobite agitation throughout the eighteenth century, and arguing that the sea-change in favour of bourgeois power only happened in the 1830s.[17] Thus, it was left to a handful of slender pamphlets to keep the Marxist flame alive. A. L. Morton, in a pamphlet published by the predecessor of the Socialist History Society, emphasised the role of an oligarchic conspiracy in the toppling of James II, whilst Willie Thompson stressed the essential 'Compromise of 1688' between the nobility and elements of the nascent bourgeoisie.[18]

Given that the left had confined itself to polemic rather than to sustained analysis, this ceded the field to the polemic, revisionist right. It also ensured that, while benefiting from the explosion of cultural history in the 1990s, the whole period we are looking at really remained untouched by the worst ravages, I would suggest, of post-modernist critique and the encroaching teleology of the free market. As the Marxists had never set up a good case for 1688, so lots of people were able to cut their careers in the 1980s and 1990s.

In the 1920s, it had been left to Hilaire Belloc to pull at the already frayed edges of the Whig consensus. Yet, his often impressionistic account of James's life, was to set the tone for many of the subsequent re-assessments of the Revolution. In his Last Rally, the advent of William of Orange—

occasioned by little more than a palace coup—led directly to all that was most disagreeable to Belloc about the modern world: industrialisation, the combustion engine, and the dominance of the Church of England.[19] He was not alone in expressing unease—if not downright distaste—for the extension of democracy that it was felt had been ushered in by the events of 1688-9. Ironically, it was left to Winston Churchill in his magnificent study of the Duke of Marlborough to restate the case for the Revolution.[20] Though undeniably partisan there is little to rival it. This is, I realise quite an indictment of both the recent historiography of the Revolution—for revolution it undoubtedly was—and of the ideological blinkers of the British left since the 1960s. At the centre of the debate there remains a yawning chasm—occasioned by the seemingly far more radical events of the English civil wars drawing away disproportionate research work, and the failure to provide a truly revolutionary analysis of what were truly revolutionary events. In Winston Churchill the grandees of what is perhaps the true 'English Revolution' found a kindred spirit in tune with their aims. 'I would—with all my heart—that the dispossessed and the hopeful, who formed the crowds of revolutionaries crowding Newcastle, Chester, and London streets in 1688-9 could only find such a supremely gifted champion.'

Bill Speck

In their papers both Professor Pincus and Dr Callow raised the subject of the tercentenary of the Glorious Revolution, and how the celebrations had been curiously muted in 1988. It seemed to me at the time that this was not due to indifference about the episode's historical significance, so much as ambivalence concerning an event which celebrated the triumph of Protestants over Roman Catholics, especially given the passions to which the rivalries of King James and King William could still give rise in those days in Northern Ireland. Nevertheless historians were then dismissive about the significance of the events of 1688-9. Revisionists such as Jonathan Clark denied that they were revolutionary, claiming continuity in the English polity from 1660 to 1832.[21] Marxist historians, from very different premises, curiously concurred. To them the significant shift in constitutional history had occurred in the genuinely revolutionary years between 1642 and 1660.

I had literally a vested interest in the tercentenary proceedings as I published a book that year with the title *Reluctant Revolutionaries: Englishmen and the Revolution of 1688*. One of my motives for writing it was to cash in on the celebrations. Although it was on the whole reasonably well received one telling criticism was that I had not done full justice to the Revolution since I had concentrated on England and had said little about events in Scotland and Ireland.

My excuse then was that, in comparison with the historiography of the English Revolution, there had been relatively little research on the Scottish or Irish revolutions, even though there were vast repositories of archival material, at least for Scotland. When I wrote to the keeper of manuscripts at the National Library of Scotland for information on its relative holdings he replied 'the amount of material relating to the political history of the 1680s is so enormous that unless you can be a great deal more specific about what you want to see there is really very little that I can do to help you'. I published this reply in a footnote to explain why I had backed off an investigation of the Scottish revolution, which led some critics to rebuke me for not having examined these sources. In fact there was no way I could have got sufficient study leave to cope with them. To me it is an indictment of Scottish historians of the late Stuart era for neglecting to engage in the research necessary to establish the most basic historical context for that period in the history of Scotland. This appears to be still very much the case. When Tim Harris came to work on the 1680s the only substantial secondary work he could cite on the subject was an unpublished Ph.D. thesis by Kathleen Mary Colquhoun completed in 1993 at the University of Illinois.

In his two volume work on the 1680s, *Charles II and his Kingdoms 1660–1685* and *Revolution: The Great Crisis of the British Monarchy 1685–1720*, Harris approaches the Revolution from the perspective of all three kingdoms, England, Scotland and Ireland.[22] This approach undoubtedly pays dividends. Thus Harris shows how events in one impacted on the other two. The Jacobite Charles Leslie claimed in 1692 that it was James II's showing favour to the Irish Catholics that

> brought upon himself all his misfortunes. Putting them into Power, and displacing Protestants to make Room for them, made more Noise, and rais'd K[ing] J[ames] more Enemies, than all the other Male administrations, charg'd upon his Government put together.[23]

Above all the promotion of the Catholic earl of Tyrconnell to the post of Lord Deputy put the wind up the English. It prompted Lord Wharton to compose 'Lilliburlero' which he later boasted had 'sung a deluded king out of three kingdoms'. As for Scotland, James's daughter Princess Anne observed in June 1688 'what has been done there has been a forerunner of what in a short time has been done here.'[24] William of Orange's Declaration spelled out his charges against James's misrule of Ireland, which was 'in the hands of papists', and Scotland, which had been 'robbed of her liberty', as well as in England.

Valuable though the three kingdoms approach is, it could be claimed that it does not go far enough. If we are to put the Revolution in the context of James II's dominions then surely the American colonies should be included. Colonial historians have established the phenomenon of the Glorious Revolution in America. David Lovejoy published a book with that title as long ago as 1972. Yet it has not been absorbed into the mainstream of Stuart historiography. Perhaps it is felt that the colonies were too remote to have a significant impact on events in Britain. Yet though they occurred 3000 miles away across the Atlantic Ocean, developments in America were viewed as relevant to those in the mother country. 'All men take as the just modell of government in New York' observed William Penn in 1680 'to be the scheme and draught in little of his [James, duke of York] administration of old England at large'.[25] James was then proprietor of New York which he ruled arbitrarily through his deputy Sir Edmund Andros. Thus he refused requests for a representative Assembly, observing that it would be 'of dangerous consequence, nothing being more known than the aptness of such bodies to assume to themselves many privileges which prove destructive to, or very oft disturb, the peace of the government wherein they are allowed.'[26] Although he reluctantly gave in to demands for an assembly in 1683, after he became king, and New York became a Crown colony, he suppressed its meetings.

Indeed he showed his aversion to representative bodies elsewhere in the colonies even before he succeeded to the Crown. As the king's brother he advised Charles II to revoke the charter of Massachusetts in 1684 and to take that colony under his direct control. As James II he incorporated Massachusetts, Rhode Island, New Haven, Connecticut and New Hampshire into the Dominion of New England. Andros was appointed as Governor and proceeded to rule arbitrarily, raising taxes by decree and suspending town meetings. As Richard Johnson concludes 'in the eyes of New Englanders the Dominion steadily assumed all the trappings of a despotism. Besides a "standing army" of English soldiers, censorship was imposed on the press, and men committed to prison without benefit of bail or jury trial'.[27]

The American colonies provide not only a test of James II's arbitrary notions of kingship but also of his commitment to religious toleration. Andros was instructed to implement a policy of toleration for all sects throughout the Dominion of New England, which by 1688 included New York and New Jersey. It has been claimed that in England James promoted toleration as a prelude to the conversion of the English to Catholicism. Such an interpretation could not possibly be applied to his policy in the Dominion, where Catholics were a negligible proportion of the population. It seems therefore that the king was genuinely committed to religious toleration and did not implement it to advance a Catholic agenda. This did not prevent opponents of the Dominion claiming that there was nevertheless a conspiracy to advance the Catholic cause on the part of Andros and his deputies Thomas Dongan, who was a Catholic, and Francis Nicholson, who was accused of being one. But there was so little genuine 'Popery' in the Dominion that its opponents were driven to accuse the governor of being in league with France to impose Catholicism on the American colonies. This was a hollow claim, as the main motive for consolidating colonies into a Dominion in the first place was to improve defence against the French.

The only English colony where Catholics were a prominent element in the population was Maryland. However this was not under the jurisdiction of the Crown. Maryland was a proprietary colony which had been granted by Charles I to the first Lord Baltimore, head of the Calverts, a Catholic family, as a haven for his co-religionists. By the 1680s, however, the majority of Marylanders were Protestants. Nevertheless control of the colony remained in Catholic hands. The third Lord Baltimore confined the Council to Catholics and sent a Catholic deputy William Joseph to Maryland in 1688. When Joseph arrived he addressed the Assembly on the divine right of kings. The majority of Assemblymen were Protestants, who objected to being harangued by Baltimore's deputy. They formed a Protestant Association to resist Joseph and the Council.

One reason why Baltimore stayed in England was that he was well aware that it was necessary in order to retain his proprietorial authority. This was under attack from no less a quarter than the Court. James issued a *quo warranto* against Maryland shortly after he became king. He also issued one against Pennsylvania, whose proprietor was William Penn. Penn too stayed in England at this time, appointing as his deputy John Blackwell, an old Cromwellian soldier, in order to protect his proprietary interests in America. This demonstrates that colonial politics were not remote affairs, played out across the Atlantic. On the contrary, they plugged directly into the political intrigues at Court. Penn exploited this not only to see off the threat to Pennsylvania but also to take advantage of James II's move towards the dissenters in 1686. He became the most influential courtier as far as the American colonies were concerned. When Increase Mather sought to take advantage of the king's new leniency towards dissent to request a restoration of the Massachusetts charter, he went to England and obtained an audience with Penn.

The reaction to James II's policies in the American colonies provides another test of the causes of the Revolution in the British Isles. For although the king provoked resistance in all three kingdoms it could be argued that events in the core state of England provided the essential stimulus. Certainly there would have been no Glorious Revolution in America if one had not occurred in England. This can be tested from the timing of the uprisings against the Dominion of New England which I. K. Steele carefully plotted. Sir Edmund Andros was on the frontier with Maine when news reached him that James had fled to France. He returned to Boston, arriving there on 25 March 1689, exactly three months after the king had arrived in France. It took time for intelligence to cross the Atlantic and it was not until then that news that James had fled abroad on Christmas Eve was confirmed in Massachusetts. Thus the New Englanders who seized Andros on 18 April were well aware that the king had been ousted in England. In New York Francis Nicholson's authority as Andros's deputy was not challenged until the end of May 1689. Jacob Leisler, who opposed Nicholson's appointment of a militia office to command the fort, himself occupied it on 31 May. Nicholson then fled to England.

In Maryland too the Protestant Association acted after and not before its leader, John Coode, learned of the coronation of William and Mary in England. Although this had taken place on 11 April it was not until 16 July 1689 that Coode and his adherents took over the state house and proceeded to lay siege to Baltimore's country house, in which William Joseph had sought refuge. He surrendered on 1 August. Although Pennsylvania is not usually held to have been involved in the revolutionary events of 1689 Mary Geiter has shown how there was a coup there against Penn's deputy Blackwell in May, though he did not resign until December.[28]

The Glorious Revolution in America therefore occurred as a result of the Glorious Revolution in England. It could not have happened on its own. This suggests that without an English Revolution there would not have been one in Scotland too, while the conquest of Ireland by William III was necessitated by James II's going there following his flight to France. Although the Irish and Scottish perspectives throw light on developments in England, on the final analysis the crucial events occurred not in Dublin or Edinburgh but in London. This justifies those historians who continue to concentrate on those reluctant revolutionaries, the English, as Patrick Dillon did in his *The Last Revolution: 1688 and the creation of the modern world* which appeared in 2006.

Discussion

Chairman (Julian Hoppit)
A point that Bill Speck made about the agreement between Tony Benn and Jonathan Clark points up nicely the uncertain lessons of the Glorious Revolution. I too heard that debate on the radio and it was a love in, if you like, coming at this problem from very different perspectives. Let me, more strongly, quickly reflect upon time, place and themes in the Glorious Revolution and then hand back to our speakers.

On timing: all the speakers were more preoccupied, though this less true of what Steve Pincus said, with how far back one goes. Do you think there is a major issue here of what I would call the problem of the Restoration? Is 1660 given too much weight as a division within English and British history? What might be the value of incorporating the 1640s and 1650s within a longer-term perspective on the Glorious Revolution?

On place: I would agree with Bill's conclusion there. Though he started off by praising Tim Harris's approach, he was actually fundamentally at odds with it. There is undoubtedly value in bringing Scotland, and Ireland into the account, but, when all is said and done, William landed in England and headed straight for London. Of course Steve is right, we need to set the revolution in a comparative framework and he pointed out some similarities but he might have spoken a bit about some dissimilarities. The absence of the storming of the Bastille, for example.

This leads me to my third point about the themes of the Glorious Revolution. I might reflect upon some absences in some of the literature. Might it be argued, for example, that Tim Harris took the wrong example from John Morrill. Should he have gone for Morrill's earlier work on neutralism, the lot of the provinces and the absence of engagement rather than his more recent Three Kingdoms perspective? Was it not the positive decision not to involve themselves in high political manoeuvres, which opened the door for William's descent upon England to be successful?

The final point: I would like to know what 'modern' is? What is 'modernity' in all of this? It is pretty fluid and I'd like you to pin it down a bit.

Steve Pincus
I want to make two points, maybe three.

The first relates to Julian's comment about the absence of the storming of the Bastille and the lack of violence. In fact the only reason why we think there was no violence is because people have not done the research. Let me give you an example. One of the central events in the French Revolution, is the massacre at the Champ de Mars. How many people died in the massacre of the Champ de Mars? Fifty. How many people died at the encounter at Wincanton? Seventy eight. If you tally up the number of people killed between 1688 and 1689 in England itself, not counting what's going on in Scotland, or Ireland where there was quite a lot of violence, there is actually a higher percentage of the overall population killed than during the period 1789–91.[29] One of the great symbols of the revolution of 1789 was the tearing down of statues, mostly the statutes of rivals. One of the primary events—and somebody mentioned Newcastle—in the revolution of 1689 is the attack by the mob which tore down and literally decapitated the statue of James II in Newcastle. There was massive violence on the streets, there were massive attacks on property and there was expropriation of property in a variety of ways. And obviously there was quite a lot of violence in Ireland and Scotland.

It is true the reason why contemporaries talk about bloodlessness is because everybody expected a full-scale civil war in England in 1689. That did not happen because of political and military decisions by James to fight the set piece battles elsewhere. But there was a lot of popular violence which is documented in eight pages of heavily footnoted material in my book, coming out next year.

The second point is about religion. Tim Harris says his book is about popular politics and the revolution in the three kingdoms but what it is really about is religion, religion in the three kingdoms and the revolution. One of the central misconceptions is about the nature of James's Catholicism. It is assumed that James was a Catholic, England was a Protestant country, that there was anti-Catholic sentiment—and there was. But, later seventeenth-century European Catholicism was rent by a violent division between French style Catholicism and, lets call it, Papal Catholicism—and that's shorthand. And there were deep, deep divisions within the English, Irish, Scottish and colonial Catholics communities. James was reconciled to the Catholic church by a French Jesuit. All of his close associations at court supported a French style of Catholicism which emphasised absolutism, which emphasised intolerance and this is the point. If you actually read the Catholic apologetic coming out of James's court, it is not a defence of toleration. It takes an Augustinian position on the Donatist controversy.[30] There is the massive translation of Bossuet's works which say, 'Yes, we should try to persuade them in the first instance, but if you cannot persuade them, there might be some unfortunate use of violence which might become necessary.' Translating Bossuet's work and other Gallicans, and publishing Bossuet's work, untranslated because it got out more quickly indicates the limits of

James's commitment to a certain kind of toleration. Lord Baltimore for example, is in the circle of the *papal nuncio* opposing James's regime.[31] And Father Peter confronts the *papal nuncio*, Dada in Whitehall Palace and says, 'You are a Whig.' and Dada says, 'If to accept limits on royal authority is to be a Whig, then I am a Whig.'

These divisions and the massive amounts of money going into William's camp in 1688, from the English Catholic community which was more ultramontanist in position, is something which is not mentioned by Jonathan Israel.[32] There are lots and lots of continental style, that is to say non-French style, Catholics who come over in William's army and take up arms in England. There were just as many Catholics in William's army in Ireland as there were Catholics in James's army in Ireland. It is important to note that, while it is true that on the ground there were not many Catholics in the dominion of New England, the army and the militias in New England were headed up by a Catholic, Colonel Dongan, who was reconciled to the Church by another French Jesuit. Bungden was rapidly Catholicising the militia in New England, giving rise to serious fears of intolerance.

John Callow

In terms of how far back we go: I think, if you are teaching you like dates, you like watersheds. 1660, 1688 or 1689 are obvious ones. But I think a central problem was the creaking Elizabethan taxation system, which got Charles I into so much trouble. How do you actually pay for a state that wants to do all that states do, that wants its colonies, that wants a big army?

When we lament, perhaps, the lack of blood-red revolution in these years, we need to look at what kind of resistance was available to people: how resistance was constrained. And one of the problems, I think, in terms of making revolutionary change at this period, is the professionalisation of the armed forces; the art of war is becoming a lot more complicated. So a recourse to arms, I suggest—is getting, especially after Monmouth's defeat, and Monmouth's defeat highlights it—incredibly difficult.[33] When we look for it, it's sporadic but those crumbling monuments all around lowland Scotland, which are now turning to dust, do reflect an ongoing civil war in all three kingdoms that bled on and on and on from 1666 onwards and was never entirely put down right up until the revolution of 1688–9.

I come to the bronze statue. It was the biggest equestrian statue built up till that time in Britain. I don't know if there ever was a bigger one. If you go to Newcastle the church bells are actually made out of the bronze that the townsfolk threw into the river when they chopped up the statue. The town regretted it about thirty years later and sent down divers and got the pieces up. Being good Whigs and moneymen, they smelted them, and made themselves a nice set of bells. But at the time the statue was torn down, the soldiers were playing a big role in organising the crowd, buying drinks for the people along the quayside. One of the depositions in the state papers talks about an NCO going out and throwing money to the crowd to egg them on until they begin to break the stirrups off the statue of James.

So, there is the role of the army and the difficulty of actually effecting radical change. It is true that there are Whig intelligence networks in London and there is a Whig underground, which is quite potent. But how to actually effect a revolution, without external help, without a recourse to military training is I think a lot more difficult in the period we are looking at, maybe, even than it was in the 1640s.

As for modernity something big and interesting happens in the seventeenth century, something massive. People's mindsets alter in very definite ways from the middle years of the century to the late years. For instance, if we were to go out now, out to Tottenham Court Road, and run into Francis Bacon or the London puritan artisan Nehemia Wallington, who also kept biographical notes and then, ten or twenty minutes, later run into Samuel Pepys, I guess our perceptions, our way of looking at the world, our interests, would tally quite nicely with Pepys. That is why he is still read today. That is why he is easy, entertaining reading because the individual is in the forefront: the individual's reactions to something he has seen—to a pretty girl, to the latest china brought in from the East India Company; we have no similar accounts from Pepys after 1669, because he is worried about his sight going. But that sense of description—a product of the individualisation of society—is exactly what is missing from Wallington's work.[34] What he cares about is not the pretty girl, not the china. It's the drowned and the saved. 'Am I damned? Is my wife going to be damned? Are my daughters going to be damned?' And I think a shift from an overwhelmingly theocratic view of the universe to something which is recognisable today is a major cleave in intellectual history.

Bill Speck
I'd like to pick up two of Julian's three points.

The timing: I think you are right. It is important and, of course, you cannot begin in February 1685. The events of the central decades of the seventeenth century loom very large over this whole period and it's a cliché to say Charles II never forgot that he had a joint in his neck. Of course he didn't. But I wonder whether, as Steve says, we were on the brink of civil war. I am sure people feared it but whether they were on the brink of it or not, is a different question. It seems to me that the forces of inertia behind the regime, however far it pushes its luck, were immense, because people shared an almost Hobbesian view that anything was preferable to going back to that nightmare. Anything. Now, at the end of the day, they were prepared to risk the nightmare again, because James proved that some things were preferable. So far from the seventeenth century perpetuating revolutionary fervour in England, however, it's quite the reverse; a generation did not want to live through its fathers' generation. And that's what the Revolutionary Settlement is all about. There is huge inertia behind the regime.

On religion: Yes, I agree that James is ambivalent in his religion; certainly his attitude towards the Huguenot refugees following the revocation of the Edict of Nantes swings hot and cold. He is probably inclined towards agreeing with Louis XIV's policy if not his methods, but as a *politique*, more reluctantly perhaps, he tries to be more accommodating. Yes, Dongan was a Papist but he was replaced, wasn't he, by Nicholson when word got back that he was a Catholic, because James did do a u-turn on Catholic appointments in 1688, when he saw how unpopular many of them had become.[35] And you have got to say that James was totally sincere in the Declaration of Indulgence [1687] where he says he was ever against persecution because of its consequences, not least of which was it disturbed trade. And I think he was sincere, at that stage. So I still come back and say, that for all his private inclinations and, you are absolutely right, that he is a bigot in many respects, publicly he does not subscribe to those attitudes.

And finally, the question, the fundamental point that Steve made at the very beginning, that it is not traditionalism versus modernism but it is two views of modernising. And I think the way he postulates it—the two models, the French model which absolutely is the bang up-to-date way you run a state if you are doing it centrally, as a model, and the Dutch model, which is a very different republican model, these are two views of modernity, and I am persuaded by that argument.

Tim Hitchcock
What really surprised me about the presentations was the extent to which they did not seem to engage with contemporary politics, with modern politics, in the way that one thinks about political history having done so, particularly on the left, over the course of the last couple of centuries. And it struck me as very surprising that nobody was really, well, with the exception of Bill Speck to some extent and in a limited way, willing to stand up and say that there are things like the politics of devolution and the politics of the break up of the nation state, which was in some ways created in 1688

and through which we can understand it. I just wonder if you could try to locate the different analyses that we have heard in that more contemporary frame.

Speck
I suppose John did address the contemporary relevance of the…

Hitchcock
Well my feeling was that Tim Harris was given a kicking, quite a bit. In a sense his three kingdoms model was precisely a dialogue with contemporary British politics; but certainly in a way that reflects the American propensity to see the settlement of 1689 as the beginnings of intellectual tradition that justifies a particular kind of enlightenment state. Maybe this isn't relevant in a British context.

Pincus
Well, can I just say something very narrowly on the British problem. I actually spent two years of this project working in the Scottish archives and the reason why I don't talk about Scotland in the book is because it undergoes a different revolution and I don't think Tim does it justice. I think he gets 90 per cent of what he says about Scotland wrong; there was a revolution in Scotland, but it was a very different thing.

Now let me say something about the contemporary issues. It strikes me that a number of our contemporary debates are about imposing modern western values on different parts of the world. Obviously there are debates about what those values are. If one does not see modernity as unitary and that there are competing versions of what the modern might be, it would lead one to have different kinds of views about international relations. One of the central tropes which struck me about the Cold War was Walt Rostow's version of modernisation[36] which said that modernisation leads ineluctably to democracy and a neo-liberal state. Part of what I am saying is that there were multiple patterns of modernity. They do not lead ineluctably in that one direction, and one should be extremely cautious about imposing certain kinds of visions of democracy or freedom on other parts of the world.

Callow
I am just going to say, I wish to God we did have an enlightenment state! But never mind!

I am very much taken with the what Steven said about multiple patterns of modernity. What I was trying to say in the course of the introduction was something about the perils of trying to impose a view of history that is to an extent moralising, and is to an extent wish fulfilment on the past. I think what you ought to be led by is the primary sources. The modern can inform, the modern can shape but the past is a very, very different world. If we look at other disciplines; recent anthropology, as I understand it, is trying to abandon 'modernity' and look at other societies in their own terms. I think we should do that with the seventeenth century. Our...concepts... you know, go into blind alleys: simply looking at 1688 in terms of what contemporaries thought about revolution probably gets you a bit further.

Simon Renton
To come back, Steve, to your competing forms of modernity, one of which you characterised as essentially based upon wealth creation and land holding, the other of which you characterised as being based upon an idea of wealth creation out of manufacture and commerce.

Pincus
Yes.

Renton
Now, it seems to me that in most understandings of modernity, ideas of wealth and consequent political power that are based upon land, are normally characterised as being rather un-modern. And, that those that are based upon other sorts of manufacture and commerce tend to be characterised the other way. Could you just unpick that for me?

On John's point I quite accept, obviously, that the past is a foreign country of which we know little. I am not entirely sure that our understanding of it is necessarily clarified by being driven entirely by the primary sources, unless we approach them with some kind of model.

Pincus
When I talk about land versus labour both are shorthand. I don't believe that there was something called a landed interest in any coherent form. What I am talking about is a way of understanding the way economies work, whether one sees the economy as infinitely expandable or one sees strict limits to what there is. One can have a very modern conception of the economy in which there are limits to development. For example, some countries see various resources as being fundamentally limited—witness their struggles for oil—but most of them are probably modern. I don't think attachment to land is something just beyond hunter gatherer society. I also accept

that there were all sorts of differences over the idea that the land imposed limits—or that there was some divinely created limit (which I would track back to the seventeenth-century language)—to what was possible.. Others see no limit. There was a very real debate in this period going back at least to the 1650s and it continues well into the eighteenth century. This can be seen, for example, in the context of the excise crisis of 1733 when much of the opposition Whig literature cites various passages from Locke's *Second Treatise*. He asserted the infinite nature of resources arguing that the focus should be on labour.[37] This gets back to the fundamental importance for our interpretation of not just focusing upon the long-term causes of the revolution but also on the long-term consequences. This is another failing of a lot of the standard historiography which stops in 1690–1.

Chairman
The poverty of empiricism?

Callow
Well, I think one of the good things about the way 1688–9 has been dealt with, as I said in my opening, is the fact that the tendency to abandon sources entirely hasn't really happened. There are historical schools at the moment, lots of periods where essentially nobody bothers to look at primary sources. Now, of course you are right, you do need a framework to interpret things, you need some kind of yard stick. What that yard stick is, stands and falls on your political persuasion, on what you are looking at, on what works best for your subject or an amalgam of different disciplines, but I think, fortunately, that is up to every body in this room to pick their own. It stands or falls on whether it kind of works or not.

Speck
The question of what is the relevance of 1688, is the absolute jackpot question. I think it is the duty of historians to show that the past is relevant, otherwise governments will stop paying us [laughter]. I think one of the ways it is relevant—and it isn't, 'What lessons does 1688 hold for us today?'—but rather how we reassess its significance in light of our experience. One of the things that is different, is that the priorities of the past generation were not those of our own generation and we need to try to work out how that has come about. How have we moved from a set of priorities in 1688, to a different set of priorities in the twenty-first century. And I would not agree with John entirely that it is up to each individual to formulate the questions. On the contrary, I think the questions, the implicit questions we have all been asking

tonight are part of the historiography. I might make the point, that in 1988 we were not concerned with long-term causes, they were at a discount, We were concerned with what were the immediate causes of the revolution. And this was all part of the great historiographical debate, about what were the causes of the English revolution, between the Marxists and Revisionists. And that has moved on. The questions that Steven is asking about the revolution of 1688 are todays' questions. They are not the questions of 1988…and I think this is the way you know what questions to ask of the sources in the first place… You cannot go to an archive, sit there and start looking and asking, 'What does this mean? Who is writing to whom? What is he saying?' You have got to go along with some questions to ask the documents. And those questions change as historians move forward in their priorities.

Chairman

There are quite a few people who have caught my eye. We need to be brisk, so,

David Parker

I will be brisk, but I could not let this moment of agreement about two models of modernity pass, having invested so much of my time in trying to demonstrate there was nothing very much modern about French Absolutism.[38] I think you are underselling your case in a way Steve, by conceding that there is a great deal modern about the other model. You are absolutely right about the two models, I am sure of that, but there is so much that is retrograde, conservative, restorative about the absolutist model, that I really think you concede too much. That does of course lead into a difficult problem about how you define modernity. Here, I think, we do have to take the past at its own assessment of the situation; because if you read Locke and all the lesser people, although they do not use the word 'modern'—at least in our sense—they were very clear that the regime of Louis XIV was not fit for purpose and I think the eighteenth century proved that to be the case. Without trying to impose any modern definitions on modernity at all, you can make that case.

I am slightly surprised at how critical you were of the existing historiography about the consequences of 1688. When, as a French historian, I came to look just at the secondary literature, in order to establish the case I have presented in short to you, I was amazed at how much there was from which you could deduce that England, in the eighteenth century, was a modern state with a modern financial system. The stuff about the financial revolution goes back years and years and years to when I was a student, and much more has been done since. Now maybe, and this is may be the point you want to make, it does not connect up to 1688 in quite the way you want to do, but the material, it seems to me, is certainly there. There is even a book called, *The First Modern State*, with a whole load of essays in it—and I have forgotten who did that now—but there was quite a lot of stuff, which did not make it too difficult to establish this comparative model.

Pincus
Lots of the historiography talks about the modernity of the eighteenth-century state. My point is that the historiography says that this is an unintentional consequence of 1688, introduced by William from outside, imposing Dutch models. The argument I am making is, that there is a big debate within England before 1688, about these competing models. My argument is that looking at the origins of the financial revolution, simply in 1694 is far too short sighted.

There is quite a lot of the literature which refers to the revolution in foreign policy in 1688–9, but that all says that the revolution in foreign policy happened afterward, that there was no discussion beforehand. I take your point about that literature.

Now, my view about modernity, I confess is informed by theoretical literature, from what used in the US to be called Sovietologists, critical of the Rostow model—which said that the Soviet state was not modern. So I am thinking here of Jerry Hough on the Soviet state who says that to think about the Soviet state as anything other than modern is deeply problematic.[39] And that in some ways, informs works by French historians like Robert Descimon who similarly talks about the French absolutists, as sort of modern.[40] What I mean about modern is bureaucratic, of maximum development of the navy, of the army. James II after all conducts the first political survey in England. These are modern things. I should say, that not only am I using this term, but a lot of James's apologists used the term to describe what they were doing as modern. So this is not an a-historical position.

James Livesey
I would suggest to the panel that in France the population does not accept the deal offered by the élite in the Revolution—but they resist not by violence—that's not the key thing but by not paying their taxes. They don't pay their taxes for five years. And, second, you get a massive transfer of the land rights. The peasantry are the gross winners of the French revolution. Thirty per cent of French land is directly owned by peasants and 50 per cent owned by peasants between 1789 and 1825. The absence of an English

peasantry makes the 1690 moment different. It provides the context for the playing out the ideological issues.

Pincus
One of the points that I have made in the theoretical stuff I have written on revolutions, is to say that there has been a fetishisation of the French Revolution, as the only model of modern revolutions. The brilliant book by Said Arjomand[41] on the Iranian revolution points out the inadequacy of that model, and Theda Skocpol, herself, is completely unable to explain the Iranian Revolution using this French model.[42] Most Chinese historians have also pointed out how she fails in her description of China. The model she uses about China in the beginning does not fit with the empirical material she provides. So the problem here is that one should not see the French revolution as the only model of revolutions, or as the primary model of revolution. One should think about a wide range of revolutions and think about commonalities. I think you are right, there needs to be ideological contestation, and there needs to be ideological contestation about the state of society and the relationship between state and society. I think that does happen in the 1690s and into the eighteenth century. I think your social description of the difference between English society and French society is exactly apt, but it is not the case that Iranian society or Cuban society was like French society, and that is a real problem, because of the tyranny of a French revolutionary model.

Callow
Very quickly to think about contested space not just in the 1690s but the 1680s. Almost every kind of public office was fought over, ideologically, with the corporation of the City of London being the major one. Why do the Whigs step on the Africa Company? Because it has got James's people in to keep the Whigs out. Why does James interfere in the Hudson Bay Company? Because he wants rid of the Whigs who came in there with Shaftesbury. Why did James taken action to prevent the election of the Whig gentleman Thomas Player to the executive of the London artillery company? Because there are Whigs drilling on the artillery field.[43] It's the same from top to bottom, even, taking a municipality like Preston: this was riven between Whigs and Tories, jockeying for the most minor positions, very often parish constables.

There was an increasing sensitivity. In the case of the artillery company they had to fight 'Carthaginians' against 'Romans', because nobody wanted to be considered the disloyal party. That is just one thought about the polarisation of society which goes on in the 1670s right through until after the revolution.

Speck
I was just thinking about what ideological slogan from 1688 can compete with the 'Rights of Man', and I think its hard to say. 'Liberty and property', has emerged hasn't it, as the slogan certainly of the Whigs after 1689. And this is rather different, isn't it, from the ideology at least as symbolised by the battlers on the rival sides in the Civil War? As I remember, Charles I's banner had on it, 'Give Caesar his due' which is like, 'Rectify the anomaly!'... but the Parliamentary one said, 'God with us' and had about four or five bibles underneath it. The difference between 'God with us' and 'liberty and property', perhaps sums up the ideological difference from one to the other.

Nancy Liveridge
Steven, I was interested in what you said about violence in the French revolution, and in particular that the number of people killed in 1688–9 was more than those killed in 1789–91. But we need to go later than 1791 to start seeing real revolutionary violence in France. I wasn't actually that sure about the violence on the streets of England; there was violence on the streets of England throughout almost the whole of the eighteenth century. But it's quite hard to identify as revolutionary *per se*, and I am not sure that the kind of ideologies you suggest would tie that in with that sort of violence.

Pincus
Obviously, the Terror is somewhat fundamental to thinking about the French revolution...but...it strikes me that there is a similar kind of ideological Puritanism (in the twenty-first century sense), of seeking ideological purity. If you look at the rhetoric around the circulation of the Association in 1696, which claimed that William was the rightful and lawful king and which something like 80 per cent of adult males actually signed, there is quite lot of discussion about what was going to happen if you did not sign it; a number of people actually, actively feared for their lives. That is one of the remarkable things about 1696, which figures so little in the historiography of the revolution. You say it does not seem like revolutionary violence, but what counts as revolutionary violence? This is something which is very unspecified in the literature, even in Rudé's book, it is not quite specified.[44]

It might be very useful to think—as Lawrence Stone said long ago—

about a long view of the revolutionary period in England from 1620 to 1722. In fact one needs to see 'the 15', and to some extent 'the 45', at last in Scotland, as a conversation about revolutionary principles. Those violent events were part of the Revolution. Similarly, it is possible to think about the playing out of French revolutionary violence not ending with the Terror but going on into the nineteenth century. It also is difficult to not think of Stalin's purges as somehow related to the Russian revolution, although it is true that there is a revisionist school of Russian revolutionary historiography which wants to stop the revolution in 1920.

Blair Worden
I'd like to ask two overlapping questions of the first two speakers, overlapping because they both have to do with left-wing conceptions of seventeenth century England. Steve, it used to be fashionable to trace 1640–60 as the first modern revolution, due to the Levellers, the Diggers, the trial and execution, the abolition of the monarchy and the House of Lords. I am wondering whether that was wrong or whether it just is that 1688 is in some way more revolutionary, revolutionary in a different way, or how you see their relationship to each other.

And second, it is not clear to me what it is, from the socialist perspective, that is wrong about Tony Benn's view of 1688. It offers a long radical pedigree behind him, when he talks of the eighteenth century as the introduction of a socially aggressive oligarchy and what is the sustained analysis being put forward and how you would correct that view?

Callow
You can put the 'glory' back into the revolution, without going down a totally counterfactual road, because we did not end up with Louis XIV's France. The revolution of 1640–49 is glitzy for historians; there are the Winstanleyans, the Diggers, the germ of primitive agrarian communism, elements that are fascinating for intellectual historians. Yet, in terms of real politics, it goes absolutely nowhere. Great for the history of ideas; yet, it does not produce change, a State that works. What you get in 1688–9 is a blueprint, which guarantees toleration. As Bill has said, James did genuinely want toleration for his subjects and this was definitely linked to his conception of trade. I think that the interesting thing about Steven's two versions of modernity is that James, in his latter days, drops down into a great hole between them…He is actually left behind…

There are profound things to celebrate on the left from 1688–9. If you want to extend the Scottish model simply consider the length of the period from the signing of the National Covenant in 1638 to the time the killing finally stopped—a pretty big one recorded in the martyrologies of the 17, 18, 19 year-old men and women who were arbitrarily killed, in the heather. So I think the Revolution is more dynamic, far more interesting and resolved much more than the traditional left view suggest. And we avoided becoming a very, very different nation as a result of a successful revolution.

Pincus
The problem with the old view is that there was a restoration of the monarchy. 1640–60, which threw up a number of interesting things but was limited in a variety of ways.. But the key thing was that Charles II and James II, not only came to power, but they constructed a different kind of absolutist regime. Nothing was inevitable about 1688–9. Christopher Hill's view that 1688–9 was the sort of afterthought is deeply problematical. I think that there was a serious modern state project going on which was moderately successful between 1660 and 1688. So the revolution of 1688–9, for various, varied reasons, made it impossible for there to be a serious kind of absolutist regime in England. That said, I don't agree with the old Whig point, that this is the only revolution; it would have been impossible for the revolution of 1688–9 to have happened without the events of 1640 and 1660. There was a significant process of state formation described by Braddick and others in the 1640s and 1650s and, for the first time in the 1650s, ideas that the economy was infinitely expandable and that labour not land was the source of property ideas were given an airing. There was a habit of discussing politics in public in this period which was creative. So, it would not have been possible to have the revolution of 1688–9 without what happened between, 1620 and 1660. But the problem with the old view is that the restored monarchy was a serious thing. It wasn't an afterthought and it wasn't, above all, a return to the way things were under Charles I.

John Seed
Talking about how far back to go, it struck me that Margaret Thatcher was elected twenty eight years ago this month. That's the gap from the Glorious Revolution to the Restoration. And, going back as far as the execution of Charles I, would take us back to 1968. It seems to me there is a danger in discussing how far back we go just in terms of state building, long-term economic, political processes. There were people who lived through that and are part of what is going on in 1688–9; the settling of scores, anger, bitterness, resentment—'if we don't get rid of that guy he is going to kill us'. So there is a realm of experience, ideology, relationships in play here,

which do not conform to any model of state building or rather connects with it in interesting ways.

Pincus
Do you not think state building never had anything to do with settling scores?

Seed
I do, but state building does not always take the form of, 'what kind of model the state shall we have?' It's often, 'That guy has got to go. How do we get rid of him?'

Chairman
Lets finish there. We might remember that Richard Cromwell died in 1712.

Acknowledgements
Recorded by Ami Kothar, transcribed and edited by Margaret and David Parker.

Notes

1. John Millar (Professor Law, Glasgow), *An Historical View of the English Government*, Fourth Edition (London, 1818), vol.IV, p.95.
2. Robert Viscount Molesworth, *The Principles of a Real Whig* (London, 1775), pp.5–6. Originally printed in 1711.
3. Millar, *Historical View*, vol.III, pp.1–2; vol.IV, pp.78, 102–3.
4. Hume, *History* (1841), vol.VI, p.336.
5. Blackstone, *Commentaries* (1765–9), vol.I, pp.311, 314; vol.IV, pp.426–7.
6. Charles Tilly, *European Revolutions, 1492–1992* (Oxford, 1993), p.104.
7. Viscount Whitelaw, 27 March 1984, Lords Debates, HLRO, WMT/1/Pt.2.
8. Patricia Morrison, *Daily Telegraph*, 21 September 1988, HLRO, WMT/22/Pt.2.
9. Jeff Goodwin, *No Other Way Out* (Cambridge, 2001), p.4.
10. Crane Brinton, in *The Nature of Revolution* (New York, 1965 revised and expanded edn), p.3.
11. H. Ainsworth, *James the Second; or the Revolution of 1688. An Historical Romance*, 3 vols in one (London, 1848).
12. Central Office of Information, 'Parliament and the Glorious Revolution', (London, 1988), p.ii.
13. L. Schwoerer, 'Celebrating the Glorious Revolution, 1689–1989', *Albion*, 22 (Spring, 1990), pp.19–20.

14. See for example, A. MacLachlan, *The Rise and Fall of Revolutionary England. An Essay on the Fabrication of Seventeenth-Century History* (Basingstoke, 1996), pp.310–12 cf. T. Benn, *The End of an Era. Diaries, 1980–1990* (London, 1994).
15. C. Hill, *Some Intellectual Consequences of the English Revolution* (London, 1980, rpt. 1997), p.16.
16. London District CPGB, *Communist Manifesto Centenary Meeting and Pageant* (London, 1948).
17. J.C.D. Clark, '1688 and All That', *Encounter* (January 1989), p.16; and J.C.D. Clark, 'The Glorious Revolution Debunked', *Sunday Telegraph* (24 July 1988), p.15.
18. A.L. Morton and W. Thompson, '1688. How Glorious was the Revolution?', *Our History* 79 (1988).
19. H. Belloc, *The Last Rally* (London, 1940); also, *James the Second* (London, 1928).
20. W.S. Churchill, *Marlborough, His Life and Times*, 2 vols, 1933.
21. J.C.D. Clark, *English Society 1660–1832* (Cambridge, 2000), p.xi.
22. Published London, 2005 and 2006.
23. Quoted in ibid., p.101.
24. Quoted in ibid., p.145.
25. W. Penn, *The Case of New Jersey Stated* quoted in Mary K. Geiter, 'The Restoration Crisis and the launching of Pennsylvania 1679–81', *English Historical Review* cxii (1997), p.311.
26. R. Ritchie, *The Duke's Province* (Chapel Hill, 1977), pp.101–2.
27. R. Johnson, *Adjustment to Empire: The New England Colonies 1675–1715* (Leicester, 1981), pp.76–7.
28. Mary K. Geiter, *William Penn* (2000), pp.144–5.
29. See for example the papers of Paul Barrillon at Ministère des Affaires Etrangères', Paris and those of the Spanish ambassador Don Pedro de Ronquillo in the archives at Simancas. Some can be accessed in *Correspondencia entre dos embajadores* (Madrid, 1951–2).
30. The importance of the Donatist controversy and the later seventeenth century debate about toleration is now ably discussed by John Marshall, *John Locke, Toleration and Early Enlightenment Culture* (Cambridge, 2006).
31. See pp.83, 87 above for Baltimore.
32. Jonathan Israel, *The Anglo-Dutch Moment* (Cambridge, 1991).
33. The Rebellion of 1685 by James Scott first Duke of Monmouth who claimed to be rightful heir to the throne.
34. David Boy (ed.), *The Notebooks of Nehemiah Wallington, 1618–1654* (London, 2007).
35. See above pp.83, 87 for Dongan and Nicholson.
36. W.W. Rostow, *Stages of Economic Growth: A Non-communist manifesto* (Cambridge, 1961).
37. Paul Langford, *The Excise Crisis* (Oxford, 1975).

38. D. Parker, *State and Class in Ancien Regime France. The road to Modernity?* (London 1996).
39. Jerry F. Hough, *The Soviet Union and Social Science Theory* (Cambridge, 1977).
40. Fanny Consandey and Robert Descimon, *L'Absolutisme en France* (Paris, 2002).
41. Said Amir Arjomand, *The Turban for the Crown* (Oxford, 1988).
42. Theda Skocpol, *States and Social Revolutions* (New York, 1979).
43. For further discussion of these episodes see Callow, *The Making of James II* (London 2000).
44. George Rudé, *The Crowd in the French Revolution* (Oxford 1959).

Books to Remember

The Glamour of Backwardness

Tom Nairn, *The Enchanted Glass: Britain and its Monarchy*, Radius, 1988

Tom Nairn's extended analysis and critique of the British monarchy in the late 1980s is unlike any other that had appeared until then or has subsequently done so. Nairn wastes little time on the royal personalities but instead engages with the function of the institution in preserving our weird and unique version of political culture. In spite of everything that has taken place in the past two decades, from royal crises to alterations in the structure of the House of Lords, the book remains no less relevant today.

Ever since the fifteenth century at least, ostentatious display has been intrinsic to the character of English monarchy, and that tradition, expanded and refined in the nineteenth century and reinforced in the twentieth by communication technology, continues unabated, 'a psychodrama which has worked'. Nairn demonstrates that the hype of glamour and celebrity surrounding the monarchy is far from being a constitutional irrelevance of no political significance 'a weirdly perverse blend of the infantile and the living dead' or a harmless Dallas-style soap opera spiced with bewitching kitsch rituals.

The suction-like grip that it is made to exert on popular consciousness —'an ideological keystone or totem'—is readily apparent, never more spectacularly than on the occasion of Princess Diana's accidental death, eerily reminiscent of the near demise (or alleged near demise) of the Prince of Wales in 1871, which was manipulated by the Establishment, with Gladstone in the lead, to kill reviving British republicanism stone dead—Nairn explains in detail how this was brought about. Today the inexhaustible interest in every trivial detail of the royal doings alongside personal identification with the family members appears to be an entrenched reality of the national culture: 'Narrow vested interests in Royalty pall before this wider acceptance and enthusiasm'. A phrase which comes readily to mind is 'cult of personality', and it does occur to Nairn, but he elaborates on it to show how this is integrated with images of domesticity, and 'A dose of naughtiness…feeds the appearance of intimacy without really threatening the faith'—a very percipient comment, especially in the light of subsequent events:

> A sort of cosiness is radiated through alienation: a warmth of belonging and self regard which no mere reality could bestow. While it lasts this organic adhesion to the whole will, like Monarchy itself, continue to eclipse all the attendant absurdity, brazen anachronism and belligerent snobbery. (p.314)

Nairn contends that this sort of thing has blocked the development of a democratic civic consciousness or authentic national sentiment. The British (Nairn terms it 'Ukanian') monarchy is essentially the creature of the dominant élites centred in south-east England whose business is landowning, commerce, finance and government. They have put their stamp upon English national identity and the monarchy exists primarily as their instrument for keeping thing that way and converting Englishness in their hegemonic style into Britishness of the same sort. Hence its cultural significance is enormous.

Nairn goes on to argue that attacking the institution on account of the personal inadequacies of its family members, its expense or its preposterous flummery misses the point and that the voices of critics up to now, whenever they dare to raise their heads, are expressed within the terms already set by monarchy itself for in these attacks no less than the acclaim the state and its history are translated into personal terms. A deeper analysis, differently conceived, is required.

The Historical Context

The British monarchy has hardly any parallel elsewhere in today's world—'the Third Millenium's single specimen of late-capitalism encased in an early-modern Monarchic Constitution'. Most other states are republics. Of those which aren't, the Scandinavian and Benelux countries' kings and queens are modest and retiring by comparison, virtually semi-commoners; the Japanese emperor was stripped of his sacral power following the country's defeat, and the few remaining absolute monarchs in Asia are of no significance or rule tiny countries.

In the early modern era England's rulers differed little from their continental counterparts and the Tudors were as absolutist as any of them, but in the seventeenth century they diverged historically. When in 1649 Charles I was physically liquidated and in 1688 his son was removed on account of their absolutist proclivities the Anglo-British ruling class of commercially minded aristocrats and patricians could see no alternative to a continuing monarchy—but ensured they established one tailored to their own requirements and convenience. One form of absolutism replaced another; it was embodied in the concept of 'parliamentary sovereignty'—a secularised version of the divine right of kings under the control of the dominant élites—with a head of state retaining some elements of sacred royalty but confined to a very limited real authority (which diminished gradually over the following centuries at the same time as his or her totemic character was enhanced). Mass democracy was a much later ill-fitting add-on. Nonetheless, this proved to be an extraordinarily powerful structure, enabling the governing élites, which avoided both invasion and revolution, to absorb into their political and social culture first the industrial bourgeoisie of northern Britain and then the emergent British working class (though not the Irish and their nationalist intelligentsia in spite of the Crown's 'mystic super-nationality').

The point regarding Ireland is important and Nairn could have made more of it to underpin his argument. At the beginning of the twentieth century, as he notes, Europe was full of royal regimes loosely modelled on the British. The Kaiser ruled over a very powerful state indeed; Germany was a homogenous national unit and therefore the German élites were in a position to develop nationalism in their support. The Habsburg Empire by contrast, like the United Kingdom was a multi-national entity, but there the emperor lacked the good fortune of his British equivalent; in the Habsburg domains there was no state nationalism, nationalism meant separatist aspirations, and that empire was being torn apart by national conflicts long before its destruction in 1918.

In the UK this feature applied only to Ireland; Scotland and Wales were well integrated into the system—by means of royalty. Nairn early on describes how in 1911 Lloyd George cynically revived the long-defunct 'investiture' ceremony for the new Prince of Wales in order to reinforce royalist enthusiasm in Welsh hearts. The wartime slogan 'Your King and Country Need You!' is more revealing than its authors intended—indicating that British patriotism is assumed to be based not on an authentic national sentiment but on an *ersatz* royally-defined version. Nairn comments that, 'The Royal passion play must be an expression of some underlying structures of British national existence'.

Broader Analysis

In his closing chapters Nairn uses his analysis of the British monarchy as a starting point to sketch one of much broader scope, where he attaches a great deal of weight in this argument to Arno Mayer's *The Persistence of the Old Regime: Europe to the Great War*. Capitalism throughout Europe (including Britain) Nairn argues, developed in the context of early modern social formations dominated by aristocratic political regimes, which continued to adapt, absorb the new economic circumstances and maintain their political hegemony—and even in France, where the revolution against them was most complete, they fought back tenaciously. Their hold in continental Europe was not finally broken until 1945—and as late as the 1970s in the case of the Iberian dictatorships.

In the UK the royal prerogative, embodied in an all-powerful prime minister, has persisted to this day as traditionalism was constantly renovated and updated without ever losing its essence, and even Thatcher' grisly career, with its Blairite parallels, has not succeeded in overthrowing that system nor uprooting royal devotion in the public consciousness, nor eliminated attempts to instil a counterfeit 'British' nationalism—one only has to listen to Gordon Brown's performances. The royal cult, the totem of the 'Greatness' in the imagined 'Great Britain', does not only sell newspapers and provide entertainment but constitutes the lynchpin of a system stretching from the honours list through the absence of a written constitution to the formal royal appointment of the cabinet, a system which poisons political and social consciousness and conceals the real face of an antiquated and malign political structure, 'an archaic institution may express something deeply and incorrigibly archaic about the society whose institution it is'.

The Enchanted Glass, though its style can occasionally be open to criticism (and its lack of an index most frustrating) was a remarkable and timely volume. It well deserves to be updated and reprinted and its arguments to be further explored and developed, for 'The Monarchy is nothing in itself but everything as part of a Monarchic Constitution'.

Willie Thompson
Northumbria University

Reviews

John Callaghan, *The Labour Party and Foreign Policy, A History* (Abingdon, Routledge, 2007), 346pp., ISBN 978-0-415-24696-5, £23.99

There has been a lot of interest in the foreign policy of the Labour Party in recent years. This is not surprising given that the party is in power and active on the world stage both diplomatically and militarily. John Callaghan's *The Labour Party and Foreign Policy, A History* is a welcome and timely addition to the recent scholarship and adds much to the debates surrounding both Labour's foreign policy and its place in a rapidly changing world. Callaghan demonstrates clearly and intelligently how Labour's foreign policy evolved throughout the twentieth century while maintaining many of its original beliefs. One of the main arguments presented here is that while Labour was in power, its foreign policy generally stuck to the same principles that had shaped its views in its early years. A 'continuity of policy...marked Labour's brief periods in Government' and Callaghan argues persuasively that a reason for this can be found in the 'origins of the party' when it accepted 'the need to represent the nation as a whole' (p.284).

Labour's desire for stability in foreign and domestic affairs is the key to understanding the party's actions both at home and abroad. Callaghan does not suggest that stability meant an overall resistance to change, but that Labour's international outlook was always defined by its belief in reformism and evolutionary change. He points out that proponents of civil disobedience in India were called upon to 'trust in the benign evolution of constitutional change devised at Westminster' (p.99). This can also be taken as a fundamental trait that shaped Labour's foreign policy for most of the twentieth century.

The book's opening chapters—particularly 'Party and Liberal nation'—argues that the forces which shaped Labour's early foreign policy were linked to traditions of radical Liberalism, rather than to a pursuit of global socialist change. Callaghan notes that the Labour Representation Committee (or LRC as the Labour Party was known until 1906) was 'not the outcome of a struggle for a socialist party' (p.1). Instead the influential socialists who helped to establish the LRC accepted that they would rely upon the support of the trade unions that were led 'by men whose disenchantment with the Liberal Party…did not entail disenchantment with liberalism' (p.1). Early assessments of world affairs were therefore made with a liberal rather than a socialist understanding. Indeed, Callaghan demonstrates clearly that by the end of the First World War, it was the Union of Democratic Control 'which exercised most influence upon the Labour Party' (p.26) and thus contributed greatly to Labour's international outlook. However, the book's focus on liberal attitudes is far from exclusive, as its extensive coverage of socialist ideas and activists also serve as a reminder that socialism was also a contributing factor when formulating policy. Callaghan makes it clear that 'Labour attracted elements aligned both with the liberal tradition of internationalism and pacifism which resisted jingoism, and, to a much smaller extent, that socialist tradition which appealed to class solidarity and working-class internationalism' (p.21).

However, as the world changed after the Great War so too did the Labour Party. Both its international outlook and domestic policies began to embrace 'socialism', a shift that came about partly because of the failures evident in the pre-war idea of a balance of power, and partly as a reaction to the Bolshevik revolution in 1917. Callaghan traces these changes well, and his focus on Labour between the wars shows how war and revolution provoked different responses from Labour's two wings. Moderate reformers favoured a pro-Wilson line which endorsed the new League of Nations, whilst the more radical socialists turned to the USSR. Both options seemed to appeal to the various strands of progressive thought inherent within the party.

After the end of the war, the hope for a better world led to support for the League from many Labourites, as it 'slotted in with those liberal convictions, so strong among Labour's leaders, which stressed the possibility of piecemeal progress in political affairs based on reason' (p.79). At the same time, there was a genuine interest in various aspects of Soviet socialism, and party leaders 'had to contend with popular and party sympathy for the struggling Bolshevik state' (p.79). After the Second World War, this choice turned into one of 'alignment with socialist and anti-imperialist movements or an American alliance that would help to defeat those very forces' (p194). It is clear from Callaghan's argument that external factors continued to play an important part in the shaping of Labour's ideas.

As well as confidently covering the main global issues that confronted Labour, the book has a fascinating strand running through it, which arises from Callaghan's obvious interest in Labour and the British Empire. Callaghan notes that many Labourites accepted the Empire as 'a force for good in the world and the basis for Britain's Great Power status' (p.21). Although critics of imperialism highlighted 'conditions of squalor, exploitation, land theft and repression' (p.91) Labour overwhelmingly subscribed 'to the official fictions of Empire' (p. 97) being 'impressed by the argument that the Empire existed, could not be erased and should be put to constructive use' (p.91). This view was challenged and to some extent erased as global events forced an updating of ideas, although the shift from pro- to anti-colonialism was not a rapid one.

The Labour Party and Foreign Policy is a well written and detailed history of Labour and international affairs and it highlights the forces that shaped the party's outlook where global affairs were concerned. If there is one thing missing, it is a discussion on how these forces presented themselves in the 'New' Labour project and their role in Tony Blair's foreign policy. Given Callaghan's ideas on the influence of liberalism, socialism and a general progressivism, it would have been very interesting to see where he placed the 'ethical foreign policy' of the early Blair years in this enlightening study of Labour's role in the world.

Jonathan Davis
Anglia Ruskin University

Alan Campbell, Nina Fishman, and John McIlroy (eds), *The Post-War Compromise: British Trade Unions and Industrial Politics, 1945–54* (Monmouth, Merlin Press, 2007), ISBN 978-0-85036-601-3, xlii+335pp., £18.95 pbk.

John McIlroy, Nina Fishman, and Alan Campbell (eds), *The High Tide of British Trade Unionism: Trade Unions and Industrial Politics, 1964–79* (Monmouth, Merlin Press, 2007), ISBN 978-0-85036-602-0, xlii+389pp., £18.95, pbk.

These companion volumes (cited below as 'a' and 'b') were first published in 1999, the fruits of a conference on 'British trade unionism, workers' struggles, and economic performance, 1940–79', at the University of Warwick in 1997. They are now reproduced in paperback with the addition of an essay (the same in each book) by John McIlroy on the critical reception of the first editions, and subsequent historiography. Both volumes follow the same format, with an introduction, thematic overviews, survey chapters by the editors, case studies (eight and seven respectively, which account for the bulk of contributions), and afterwords. Each also includes a set of useful tables, ranging from standard generalities like union density and strikes to specifics like Communist union membership and rank-and-file papers.

The era in question might be regarded as a golden age of British trade unionism, when density rose from 38.6 per cent to 52.9 per cent, one of the highest in western Europe outside Scandinavia. Insisting on free collective bargaining and rejecting the neo-corporatism which became popular in other countries, unions managed to consolidate while resisting Tory threats—famously so in respect of Heath's government—and Labour blandishments. It all began to unravel in 1979, and while that year is the termination point of the second volume, the past is usually observed through the prism of the present: hanging over the contributions (all from leftists of various hues) are the painful questions of what went wrong for old Labour, and who was responsible for the mistakes that gave Mrs Thatcher her chance?

The contributions allude to problems in three areas. First there was the inherited system of trade unionism, with its fierce sectionalism, and suspicion of paid officials. While these values had a positive side, their emphasis on 'bargain-basement principles' discouraged the creation of an infrastructure of social institutions, such as banks, newspapers and journals, sports clubs, and educational bodies, which unions in Europe managed to develop, and which expanded their relevance beyond wages and conditions. McIlroy's 'Making trade unionists: the politics of pedagogy, 1945–79', on the chronic underfunding of trade union education, is illustrative of a much wider malaise. Sectionalism also left the national centre, the TUC, relatively weak, and an organisation which enjoyed enormous prestige on the world stage in 1945 and was 'a major force in international labour circles in the years after the War' (Anthony Carew, a, p.145) was relatively ill-equipped to deal with issues at home. As Eric Hobsbawm contends in the afterword to *The Post-War Compromise*, no one 'apart from the Communists of 1941–5 [had] plans for the role of unions in post-war society' (a, p.312). For governments, unions, and employers, the compromise seemed to work. Reform of industrial relations became topical in the 1960s, but that was true of most western European countries. Inflation was now becoming a priority, and governments commonly saw tripartism and centralised bargaining as the antidote, and the rationalisation of unions as the path to industrial peace. Even in the early 1970s, public opinion was unwilling to back Heath in taking on the unions.

The second, and crucial, failure came in labour–state relations. Various authors pinpoint lost opportunities. McIlroy argues that a chance for a new departure was missed in 1944–5. Geoffrey Goodman refers to the National Union of Mineworkers' refusal to accept 'worker-management co-operation' on the nationalisation of the mines in 1947 as a 'historic negative' (a, p.27). Demonstrating that failure was a two-way process, David Howell suggests that the rot set in with the Wilson government's ineffective response 'to problems of economic and social obsolescence' (a, p.130). The proportion of trade unionists voting Labour fell from 73 per cent in 1964, to 55 per cent in the two general elections of 1974, and 51 per cent in 1979. Unions too were in camouflaged decline. Applying Hobsbawm's 'The forward march of Labour halted?' thesis to trade unionism, Richard Hyman suggests that support for unions was being hollowed out in the 1970s, and sustained by 'a substantial increase in close shop agreements' (b, p.354).

Not surprisingly, the sharpest controversy revolves around the 'winter of discontent' in 1978–9, when unions baulked at collusion with the wage policy of the last 'old Labour' government. The episode had been seen as 'a decisive historical moment when the state of the world changed and irresponsible trade unionism opened the door to Thatcherism' (McIlroy and Campbell, b, p.114). Did unions fail to anticipate a foreseeable calamity, or were they victims of James Callaghan's inability to manage the crisis of neo-Keynesianism? Without denying that the strikes gifted propaganda to Conservative opposition, the editors offer a robust defence of the unions, arguing that Callaghan's proposed pay norms of 5 per cent were hopelessly unrealistic when prices increases were topping 9 per cent that the TUC worked to establish a 'Concordat' with the government in February 1979, and that by April, Labour was again ahead of the Tories in the polls. Taking the longer view, Hyman is critical of unions for persisting with their traditional insistence on an adversarial relationship with the state. 'Pluralistic detachment', he argues, had 'run into the sands' (b, p.362). It offered no solutions and merely played into the hands of those who wished to blame the unions for Britain's economic woes. The long and the short of it are not mutually exclusive. One can fault union strategy while accepting that unions were obliged to defend real wage levels in 1978–9. And it must be said that few realised at the time that old Labour was drinking in the last chance saloon. Only in the 1980s did Thatcher's victory come to be seen as irreversible, and a key question is why it proved to be so. Other European countries experienced a similar crisis of neo-Keynesianism and a similar failure of social democratic remedies. But nowhere in Europe was the right as successful in trouncing the left in the 1980s as it was in Britain. The explanation lies partly in a malaise in the Labour movement that went deeper than the 'winter of discontent', but it lies also the politics of the 1980s.

The third focus in these volumes is the rank and file. Case studies deal with movements in engineering, shipbuilding, London bus workers, and dockers, and with militancy in the peak year of 1972. McIlroy notes the paradox that saw the ascent of British Trotskyism as the fruits of advanced capitalism percolated to the working class, and suggests that the decline of Labour and the Communists created a niche for a new generation of revolutionaries. His chapter on the topic is excellent, but ambivalent on why the impact of Trotskyists was ephemeral. On the one hand he cites generic flaws, such as the mistaken belief that state intervention, strikes, and agitation would themselves suffice to politicise workers. On the other, his conclusion that 'Dogmatism won out over creative politics and real influence in the trade unions' (b, p.285), implies a reluctance to accept that the problems lay in the medium rather than the message.

Two issues deserved greater attention. There is little on the media, apart from Goodman's very readable chapter on 'The role of industrial correspondents', and a few scattered references. The editors note the stereotyping of films like *I'm All Right, Jack* (1959) and *The Angry Silence* (1960), and their 'resonance with sections of the Conservative Party and the judiciary' (a, p.101). Yet the relentless and extensive demonisation of unions in the media had a broader resonance than that. The press villified shop stewards. Television news bulletins implied that the future of Britain hung on the outcome of the latest dispute in the car industry. Casual union bashing became a national joke, and the stuff of films like *Carry On At Your Convenience*, in which embittered little shop steward 'Vic Spanner' threatens the future of a company which has secured a big contract for the export of toilets to Arabia! The seeds of Thatcherite hegemony were already been sown.

Finally, an unacknowledged elephant in the room is the democratic deficit. It was more than a problem of oligarchism within trade unions. For this observer, at home with the flexibility of Ireland's proportional representation, the 'first past the post' electoral system forced people unnaturally into two parties, and created a dependency on managing structures rather than winning popular support. Certainly, it produced majority Labour governments, but it also meant that Labour invariably leaned to the centre and stifled the left, which was then driven into the negativity of internal opposition or the subterfuge of entryism. Union-Labour Party relations were futher compromised by the dishonesty of the card vote. Plausibly, the electoral system and the card vote provided the scaffolding which disguised the crumbling foundations of post-war Labourism and discouraged the party and the unions from doing anything about it until it was too late.

Emmet O'Connor,
University of Ulster

Gidon Cohen, *The Failure of a Dream: the Independent Labour Party from Disaffiliation to World War II* (London, Tauris Academic Studies, 2007), ISBN 978-1-84511-300-1, x+262pp., £59.50

During the ten years that 'New' Labour has been in government, a number of different socialist parties have emerged. Many claimed that they would reclaim the socialist ground left behind by 'Old Labour' and, while some succeeded in this ideologically, few have seen their efforts rewarded at election time. Gidon Cohen's *The Failure of a Dream*, which explores the trials and tribulations of the Independent Labour Party after it split from the Labour Party in 1932, acts as a valuable reminder that such factionalism has always existed within the British labour movement. He is quite right to state at the outset that the post-1932 ILP 'continues to serve as the standard cautionary tale for the left disillusioned with Labour's leadership' (p.ix).

Cohen's objective is to fill a gap in the current literature on the ILP which, as he notes, has recently focused more on the party and its relation to the key events of the 1930s (p.4). This is a worthwhile task and one that Cohen fulfils admirably. A detailed analysis of the ILP as a national body emerges, with interesting insights into the workings of regional members and local party activists being combined with the thoughts and practices of key figures such as James Maxton and Fenner Brockway. From this national analysis comes a picture of a party that both declined and grew after its split from the Labour Party. Cohen notes that the ILP in the 1930s was 'only partly a party that was decimated and destroyed by events, crises and decisions' (p.200).

The main cause of the ILP's problems was obviously its disaffiliation from the Labour Party, and this in some way highlights the fact that the divisions that have been a constant factor in left-wing politics were often most evident when pragmatist and ideologist disagreed. Cohen suggests that disaffiliation was not inevitable, with Arthur Henderson telling Brockway that matters may be sorted out more amicably if only the ILP 'would commit itself to non-revolutionary methods (p. 27). However, Cohen also rightly points out that it was 'unlikely that such a commitment would, by itself, really have satisfied the Labour Party's NEC' (p.27). It was arguably the ILP's revolutionary socialism via the Revolutionary Policy Committee that alienated mainstream Labour the most. Ironically this also alienated many ILPers as well, as such far-left ideals, together with formally breaking away from the Labour Party, was not desired by many ILP members. After 1932, many loyal ILPers left their party despite sentiments such as those of Patrick Dollan, who declared that '[w]hoever may claim to be the ILP, we in this hall are the ILP' (p.29). Cohen makes it clear that if the ILP in Glasgow 'with all its members and traditions wanted to continue on a steady course, it did not cease to be the ILP just because someone from a very different part of the country passed a ridiculous motion at the national conference' (p.29). From this came other questions that the disaffiliationists and affiliationists spent the rest of the decade arguing over.

As well as covering the 'big debates' on things such as the USSR, Spain and the Unity Campaign, Cohen focuses on smaller, but no less interesting, details like party membership and organisation, and he assesses the many problems that disaffiliation brought, such as losing a significant number of members and branches (pp.30–6). Cohen notes that some areas were hit worse than others. For example, while the Welsh Division was 'decimated' in its strongest regions, London was less affected, losing only one of eighty nine branches while seeing eight new branches formed. East Anglia also fared better than many other places, with the Norwich branch losing only 'a few paper members' as a result of disaffiliation' (p.33). A consequence of this was that areas which were 'less severely affected became relatively more influential' (p.33). Cohen also highlights the significant problems the party faced at elections when ILPers fought old comrades, sometime splitting the vote and allowing National Government candidates to win.

Other interesting aspects discussed here include the social side of being a member of the ILP and the relationship that the party developed with the Communist Party of Great Britain (CPGB). In some respects these features went hand in hand, as radical and revolutionary socialists found common ground in the shared ideas of 'the Left', although it must be noted that the fierce animosity that underpinned left-wing sectarianism was never far away, and, as was often the case, opinions could differ over the USSR. In his section on 'Activity: Social and Political', Cohen points out that a 'focus on membership helps outline some of the central issues which the ILP faced in the 1930s' (p.37) and it is noted that social events often 'had an explicitly political intent' (p.43). For example, there was 'no clear differentiation between social and political activity' that included the '*New Leader* cycling corps that would travel out to villages around Glasgow each weekend to distribute the paper' (p.201).

The Failure of a Dream is a valuable addition to the histories of the Independent Labour Party, especially as it re-examines the ILP in light of the recently opened Comintern archives in RGASPI in Moscow. It is a pity that more use was not made of documents from here, as there are more details in the files concerning the CPGB and the ILP. However, Gidon Cohen eloquently shows that the ILP did not simply fade away after it broke away from the Labour Party. Instead it continued to recruit activists and maintain a political existence that gave British socialists an alternative to mainstream Labour and the Communist party of Great Britain. This is arguably the main strength of the book as it would have been easy to simply detail the ILP's decline and ultimate fall. Instead, a fascinating picture is drawn of a political organisation that believed in itself, that tried to make full use of its powerful history but ultimately fell at the feet of its younger offspring.

Jonathan Davis
Anglia Ruskin University

Socialist History Society

The **Socialist History Society** was founded in 1992. Its members include many of Britain's leading socialist and labour historians, both academic and amateur.

The **SHS** holds regular events, public meetings and one-off conferences, and contributes to current historical debates and controversies.

The society produces a range of publications, including the journal *Socialist History*. It can sometimes assist with individual student research.

The **SHS** is the successor to the Communist Party History Group, established in 1946.

The Society is now entirely independent of all political parties and groups. It is engaged in, and seeks to encourage, historical studies from a Marxist and broadly defined left perspective. It is concerned with every aspect of human history from early social formations to the present day. It is particularly interested in the struggles of labour, women, progressive and peace movements throughout the world, as well as the movements and achievements of colonial peoples, black people, and other oppressed communities in seeking justice, human dignity and liberation.

Each year the **SHS** produces two issues of the journal *Socialist History*, one or two historical pamphlets in the *Occasional Papers* series, and newsletters.

In addition to our publications, we organise four or five lectures during the year, the annual A.L. Morton Memorial Lecture, and occasional conferences on specific subjects. There is an admission charge of £1.50 for all lectures. The **SHS** also organises and sponsors joint events and publications with other sympathetic groups.

Back numbers of many of our publications are available and a list of them can be supplied on request to Mike Squires, 50 Elmfield Road, Balham, London SW17 8AL. mikesquires@btopenworld.com

The annual subscription to the Society is:
UK full rate £20
UK concessionary rate £14
Overseas full rate £25
Overseas concessionary rate £19
Subscriptions are due on 1 January each year.

Membership from January entitles you to copies of the journal *Socialist History* as they are published, and a copy of each *Occasional Paper* published by the Society, as well as *Newsletters* on the work of the committee.

Members joining the **Society** between September and the end of the year receive the second journal of the year and their membership will continue for the whole of the following year. All members enjoy the same rights to elect and to be elected to the Committee and the Society's offices.

You can join the **Socialist History Society** via the website (www.socialisthistorysociety.co.uk); by paying your subscription at one of our meetings; or by sending your name and address together with a sterling cheque or a postal order to: The Secretary, **SHS**, 50 Elmfield Road, Balham, London SW17 8AL.